People Helper GROWTHBOOK

People Helper GROWTHBOOK

A Manual To Accompany "How To Be A People Helper"

Dr. Gary Collins

Vision House

Ventura, CA U.S.A.

The foreign language publishing of all Vision House books is under the direction of GLINT. GLINT provides financial and technical help for the adaptation, translation, and publishing of books for millions of people worldwide. For information regarding translation, contact: GLINT, P.O. Box 6688, Ventura, California 93006.

PEOPLE HELPER GROWTHBOOK

Fifth Printing, 1983

Published by Vision House
P.O. Box 3875
Ventura, California 93006
Printed in U.S.A.

Library of Congress Catalog Card Number 76-25752
ISBN 0-88449-056-4

CONTENTS

Acknowledgments

The author gratefully acknowledges the cooperation of the following publishers and individuals who have given written permission to quote from the sources listed below.

Creation House—for excerpts from Gary R. Collins, *Effective Counseling*, 1972.

McGraw-Hill Book Company—for excerpts from E. S. Shneidman and N. L. Farberow, *Clues to Suicide*, 1957.

Prentice-Hall, Inc.—for excerpts from L. M. Brammer, *The Helping Relationship*, 1973.

Psychology Today—for excerpts from Thomas J. Cottle, "Our Soul-Baring Orgy Destroys the Private Self," October 1975.

Regal Books—for excerpts from Ray Stedman, *Body Life*, 1972.

Fleming H. Revell Company—for excerpts from R. E. Coleman, *The Master Plan of Evangelism*, 1963.

Tyndale House Publishers—for excerpts from Tim LaHaye, *Transformed Temperaments*, 1973.

Curtis Wennerdahl—for reproduction of his unpublished paper "Ideas for Phone Workers."

Westminster Press—for excerpts from William Barclay's *Letters to the Corinthians* and *Letters to the Galatians and Ephesians*.

PREFACE

Most people today have problems—with their marriages, their kids, their jobs; with loneliness, discouragement, frustration, or sex. Struggling alone, many needy people would welcome an offer of assistance from someone else, but would-be helpers often don't know how to give the help, and sometimes they're not even sure what help is needed. It is true that people helping is an art for which some are more talented than others, but all of us can learn to improve our people helping skills. It is for this reason that *The People Helper Growthbook* has been written: to train people like you in the helping skills, to increase your ability to relate to other people, to make you more sensitive to others, and to assist you in becoming a more effective people helper.

There is evidence that this growthbook program really does accomplish these goals and make better people helpers. Working with high school, college, and seminary students, as well as with housewives, businessmen, school guidance counselors, and a variety of church laymen, a research team tested the exercises which appear in the following pages and showed that they can increase both the sensitivity and the effectiveness of those who want to be people helpers.*

The People Helper Growthbook (which is meant to accompany the author's book *How to Be a People Helper*, by Vision House Publishers, 1976) consists of twelve chapters, each of which begins with a Bible study and some personal exercises to be done at home. Following this, there are projects for a study group to do together. In most cases the group members begin each session together by listening to a tape.** Along with the growthbook, the tapes provide instructions on what to do in the group meeting and include some of the author's personal observations and suggestions about effective people helping. Several people have found benefit in completing the growthbook alone, without participating in a study group, but group involvement appears to be superior, and for this reason we recommend that groups of from three to twelve people study together. (When a group is larger than this, discussion tends to be

---

* Research on the people helper training program is still in progress. A complete report of the research methodology and results will be published in the near future.
** The People Helper Cassette Tapes, which cover all twelve of the study group sessions, are available from One Way Tape Library.

hindered and the participants do not benefit as much as they might in a smaller group.) Before establishing a people helper training group there are several questions which you might want to consider seriously.

1. *What is the purpose of this people helper training program?* As indicated above, this growthbook program has been written to train nonprofessional counselors in people helping skills. It is not designed to turn laymen into amateur psychologists, but it does attempt to make people more sensitive to the needs of others, more open to others, and more skilled in knowing how to help people with their problems. One way in which we can become good people helpers is to develop characteristics of openness, warmth, genuineness, and empathy. This program is designed to develop these traits in people who work through the book.

2. *What is required of the group participants?* People helping is a demanding responsibility, and there is no quick route to the development of effective people helping skills. The program which follows is challenging and demanding, but if the demands are great, so are the rewards. Each of the twelve units requires 1 ½ to 2 hours of study prior to the group meeting, and we have discovered that *people who do not do the homework do not profit as much from the program in developing people helper skills.* It is possible to limit group meetings to 1 hour for each unit, but to do so is to put the group under time pressure. It is recommended, therefore, that the groups plan to meet for a minimum of 1 ½-2 hours for each unit.

3. *Who should be in the program?* Quite frankly, a program like this sometimes attracts unstable people whose own problems might interfere with their subsequent effectiveness as people helpers. We suggest, therefore, that people should be *invited* to participate in the program, rather than opening the training sessions to everyone who might wish to be involved. The invited participants should show evidence of psychological stability and spiritual growth in their own lives, a sincere concern for other people, intelligence, and a willingness to commit themselves to a program which might take as much as 3 ½ hours of their time each week (2 hours of study plus 1 ½ hours in group interaction). In addition, the group leader should look for persons who are already being sought out for assistance and who demonstrate sensitivity and some natural or spiritual gift in helping others with their problems. It is wise to prayerfully select people as candidates for training rather than to hastily recruit anyone who will come. Such careful selection in training is important if real people helping is to follow.

4. *What is required of the leader?* Assignments for each week and the format for each study group session are printed in this book and are included on the tape cassettes. For this reason, the group leader has no responsibility for preparing lectures, nor is he or she required to be an expert in psychology or counseling skills. We have found, however, that the group leader plays a very important role in determining whether or not the program is successful. The effective leader must complete all of the assignments before the group meets, must be a good discussion leader (not inclined to dominate the group by talking too much), must be able to draw out the various group members into group discussions, and must be able to encourage the participants to complete their assignments. Use of the leader's cassette ("How to Lead a People Helper Training Group") is extremely important.

5. *What is the duration of the program?* Groups usually choose to do one lesson each week. This results in a twelve-week program. Some groups have taken a longer period of time (extending each lesson over a two-week or even three-week period), and with one group the participants completed two units each week, thus reducing the program to six weeks. Assuming that each unit takes approximately 3 ½ hours to complete, the entire program covers approximately 40-42 hours. This can be included in as little as one intensive week, or it can be spread over a much longer period of time.

6. *What problems are likely to be encountered?* In spite of the fact that the following

pages have been designed to avoid upsetting anyone, some people nevertheless find the program to be personally threatening, especially when the group is involved in practice counseling (role play) sessions. Such persons tend to drop out of the program, and in doing so they may need some help from the group leader. In the minds of many people, to drop out is an admission of failure or weakness, and such people need support, encouragement, and reassurance.

Other people will discover that the program triggers an awareness of some long-hidden or previously unrecognized personal problems. The group leader should be alert to these needs and talk with the group members, sometimes helping with the problem and sometimes making a referral to the pastor or other counselor.

Finally, there will be those who give up on doing the assignments. Many of these people may drop out of the group, but others may decide to keep attending. Such attenders do not benefit themselves, nor do they help the group. Firm but kind reminders may be necessary to help keep people involved in completing assigments. Even for those who are faithful in doing the work, frequent encouragement from the leader may be both desirable and appreciated.

7. *What can be done with the training?* We suggest that before starting a group there be some consideration of how the trainees will use their skills following completion of the program. Pastors, church elders or deacons, youth leaders, college dorm counselors, Sunday school teachers, Bible study leaders, and others who already work with people are prime candidates for people helper training. These people can use the training immediately in the groups with which they work. Others, such as teachers, medical personnel, and businessmen, have found the program to be helpful in their work, while family members might find that they can be better people helpers at home. Other ways in which the program can be used are discussed at the end of this book. The group leader may wish to read the epilogue before the training program is begun.

In developing and testing this program I have been assisted and encouraged by a number of people, to whom I am very grateful. Chief among these are my wife, Julie, and my colleague Lawrence Tornquist, whose various acts of involvement went far beyond the call of duty. Roger Parnham, James Gruenewald, Lindy Scott, and Lenora Rand all worked on the research, assisted by approximately one hundred other people who completed each of the assignments, gave their candid opinions of the program, and submitted to psychological and other testing. Georgette Sattler and Donna Brown typed the manuscript, while Arvid Nyquist efficiently reproduced and collated thousands of pages so the manuscript could be tested in mimeograph form prior to publication. Several creative and innovative pastors opened their church doors to let us test the program with members of their congregations: Arthur Evans Gay, Jr., of South Park Church in Park Ridge, Illinois; Arthur H. DeKruyter and Larry W. Rieck of Christ Church, Oak Brook, Illinois; and Roy Ackermann of Trinity Community Church, Milwaukee, Wisconsin. To all of these people I give my sincere thanks. They should not be held responsible for what follows, but their collective input has done a great deal to improve the program and make it more relevant and effective. It is my prayer that God will use this book to mold you into a more able people helper, one who will be able to touch and change the lives of people with whom you come in contact.

—Gary R. Collins

1
WHY DO YOU WANT TO BE A PEOPLE HELPER?

Many people today have problems—discouragement, loneliness, difficulty in getting along with others, lack of money, marriage and family problems, tensions, insecurity, problems at work, fear, guilt, alcoholism, etc. The list could go on for pages. Just living in our complicated society and period of history seems to create a host of difficulties; and, if we are honest, most of us would admit that we could use a little help.

But why should we want to spend our time helping each other? This is a question about our motives. Perhaps we want to be people helpers because we are compassionate, interested in people, or convinced that Christians should be loving and caring. Might it also be, however, that we are simply curious about the private affairs of other people, wanting to run other people's lives, or interested in playing the role of amateur psychiatrist? It is the purpose of this first chapter to look at our real reasons for wanting to be people helpers.

GETTING STARTED BY LOOKING TO THE BIBLE

People helping is mentioned numerous times in the Bible. Consider, for example, some of the ways in which God helps people. For each of the following, write down the ways in which God helps. The first answer is already written in.

Psalm 46:1   *The Lord helps when we are in trouble.*

Hebrews 4:16 _____

Hebrews 13:6 _____

Proverbs 3:5, 6 _____

Isaiah 40:31 _____

Philippians 4:19 _____

Very often God uses us to help others. The Bible even commands that we be dedicated people helpers. For example, look up the following and jot down what we are expected to do when people around us are in need:

Matthew 10:8 _____

Romans 12:15 _____

Romans 12:20 _____

Galatians 6:2 _____

1 John 3:17 _____

The Christian doesn't have any choice about being a people helper. Indeed, if we aren't interested in helping people it may be that we aren't even bona fide Christians (1 John 4:7, 8). A first step to being an effective helper, therefore, is to invite Christ into our lives to live there and control us.

READING

There are many people helpers around today, and they use a variety of people helping methods. You can read about them in chapter 11 of *How to be a People Helper*. Please read this carefully. It isn't the easiest chapter to understand, but it tells you what a lot of people helpers are doing and it points out some mistakes which we all can avoid.

PERSONAL EXERCISES

Let's return to the question that was raised earlier—why do you want to be a people helper? List your reasons below. Be as honest as you can and don't hesitate to include reasons that you might not be proud of.

_____

_____

_____

_____

_____

_____

_____

_____

_____

Keep adding to this list as you think of other reasons.

PERSONAL SURVEY

Good people helpers do not remain aloof and distant from others. Instead, they are compassionate, sensitive, and open with those in need. To help you examine your attitudes toward other people, please read the statements which appear below. Each is followed by a series of numbers. After reading each statement, *underline* the number which best identifies where you are on the scale. Then *draw a circle* around the number which best expresses where you would like to be.

A. In general, I am able to tell others that I really like and appreciate them.

| Not at all able | 1 2 3 4 5 6 7 8 9 | Completely able |

B. I am willing to discuss my feelings with others.

| Not at all willing | 1 2 3 4 5 6 7 8 9 | Completely willing |

C. I am able to tell a friend when I am angry about something he or she has done.

| Not at all able | 1 2 3 4 5 6 7 8 9 | Completely able |

D. I accept feedback about myself from others without responding in a defensive manner.

| Completely able | 1 2 3 4 5 6 7 8 9 | Not at all able |

E. I find it easy to relate to others.

| Always find it easy | 1 2 3 4 5 6 7 8 9 | Never find it easy |

F. I enjoy being with people.

| Never enjoy it | 1 2 3 4 5 6 7 8 9 | Always enjoy it |

G. I generally understand why I do what I do.

| Never understand | 1 2 3 4 5 6 7 8 9 | Always understand |

H. I am willing to give feedback to a friend when he or she is behaving in a way that bothers me.

| Never willing | 1 2 3 4 5 6 7 8 9 | Always willing |

I. I am a person who trusts others.

Always
   trusts   1 2 3 4 5 6 7 8 9   Never
                                                                    trusts

J. I feel free to discuss my problems and struggles with others.

Always feel   Never feel
   free   1 2 3 4 5 6 7 8 9   free

Your answers to these questions will be compared with others and discussed in the group meeting.

MEETING TOGETHER

In this first meeting, chairs should be placed in a circle, and we will start by getting to know each other. Each person should give his name and one or two facts about himself (where he is from, where he works, what he is studying, etc.). Try to learn everybody's first name. Then, as a group, listen to the tape. (It takes about ten minutes to play.)

1. After listening to the tape, each person should share his or her list of reasons for wanting to be a people helper. If your group is small, each person should share with the whole group; if the group is larger, divide it into smaller groups of six to ten people each.

After going over the lists, discuss what are good reasons and what might be poor reasons for being in the program. Ask yourself (and perhaps the group leader or group members) whether you really should stay in the group. Take about fifteen minutes for this whole project.

2. Each group member should look at the statements that were read and responded to at home. Discuss the following:

A. How does each of these statements relate to people helping?
B. How will your responses to the statements influence your ability to help others?
C. What could you begin to do to change the way you are, so that this will more closely match the way you would like to be?

Be sure to allow enough time for the following exercise. If you wish, the group may break down into groups of two or three persons each to discuss these questions.

3. Is it possible to be too open? Read the following quote from *Psychology Today** and discuss it together.

> But if there is a need to reveal, there is also a need to protect and withhold. Cards can properly be played close to the chest. We make a mistake in forcing people to believe that every secret and sentiment, every inner inch must be exposed. Freedom of speech should not be confused with perpetual openness.
>
> A new class of professionals and profiteers devoted to self-revelation are creating a world without personal protection. A world without fences, shower curtains, clothes. A world of eternal light, without shadows or night.
>
> But some of us prefer to hold onto a few secrets. We fear the ethic of publicness will strip away our privacy and individuality.

---

* Thomas J. Cottle, "Our Soul-Baring Orgy Destroys the Private Self," in *Psychology Today*, October 1975, pp. 22, 23, 87.

DISCUSSION QUESTIONS

1. Were there any parts of the reading that you didn't completely understand? Were there parts with which you disagreed? Share these with the group.

2. Can somebody explain what is meant by directive, permissive, and interactional approaches to counseling? What do you think is good and bad about each of these?

3. Many Christians believe that the Bible has the answer to all human problems. Do you agree? Give reasons for your answer.

4. Chapter 11 in *How to Be a People Helper* contains these words: "To be a Christian helper is not a task to be taken lightly. It is a committing of oneself to the challenge of being God's instrument for changing another person's life." Are you ready and willing to train for this task? Share your answer with the group.

WHERE DO WE GO FROM HERE?

When you leave the group, look over your list of reasons for learning to be a people helper and think back to the group discussion. Within three days decide whether you want to stay in the group. If your answer is no, please tell the group leader. If your answer is yes, determine to be at every training meeting and make up your mind to do the homework before each session.

EXTRA ASSIGNMENT

If you want to do some extra work, read pages 41-64 in Jay Adams' *Competent to Counsel* (Grand Rapids: Baker Book House, 1970).

2
ARE YOU SERIOUS ABOUT THE GREAT COMMISSION?

More than any other person who lived, Jesus was a people helper. He helped people with their spiritual problems, psychological hangups, interpersonal squabbles, and physical needs. At first glance, therefore, it might seem surprising that when He met with His followers shortly before going back to heaven, Jesus didn't say anything to them about helping others. Instead, He left them with a responsibility to make disciples. Might it be, however, that as a compassionate people helper, Jesus recognized that making disciples could be one of the best ways to help others? Could it be that the true disciple who is busy making disciples of others will be a people helper automatically?

In this chapter we want to explore these ideas—to think about discipleship—and to show how the Great Commission influences the ways in which we help one another.

GETTING STARTED BY LOOKING TO THE BIBLE

The Great Commission is found in Matthew 28:18-20. Try to read this in a modern translation or two. Notice that the emphasis is not on the word *go*. It is on the command to make disciples. Verse 19 would be stated accurately if it read, "wherever you are going you should *make disciples.*"

But what does it mean to make disciples? There are two parts to this task, parts which are identified by the verbs in the middle of verse 19 and the beginning of verse 20.

What are these verbs? _____

What do you think is implied in the word "baptizing"? _____

_____ (If you don't know, please see chapter 1 of *How to Be a People Helper.*) How does this apply to you personally? _____

_____

In Matthew 4:18-22 we read about Jesus' selection of His disciples.

1. What kind of people did He call? _____

_____

Does 1 Corinthians 1:26-29 help in your answer? What does this say about you as a disciple and

discipler? _____

_____

2. How did Jesus call His disciples (see Matthew 4:19)? _____

_____

Do you see any evidence of arm-twisting or forcing people to be disciples?_____

_____

3. What did Jesus promise His followers? Look up the following and write how each
could apply to you as a disciple.

Matthew 4:19 _____

_____

Luke 9:23 _____

_____

Luke 14:33 _____

_____

Discipleship is costly, but the benefits are great and the disciple of Jesus Christ possesses
what psychologist Gordon Allport has called "incomparably the greatest psychotherapeutic
agent . . . something that professional psychiatry cannot of itself create, focus, or release."[*]
What is this something? See John 13:35.

_____

READING

Please read the following descriptions of how Jesus selected His disciples.[**]

It all started by Jesus calling a few men to follow Him. This revealed immediately the direction His evangelistic strategy would take. His concern was not with programs to reach the multitudes, but with men whom the multitudes would follow. Remarkable as it may seem, Jesus started to gather these men before He ever organized an evangelistic campaign or even

---

[*] Gordon W. Allport, *The Individual and His Religion* (New York: Macmillan, 1950), p. 90.
[**] From R. E. Coleman, *The Master Plan of Evangelism* (Old Tappan, New Jersey: Fleming H. Revell, 1963), pp. 21-24. Used by permission.

preached a sermon in public. Men were to be His method of winning the world to God.

The initial objective of Jesus' plan was to enlist men who could bear witness to His life and carry on His work after He returned to the Father. John and Andrew were the first to be invited as Jesus left the scene of the great revival of the Baptist at Bethany beyond the Jordan (John 1:35-40). Andrew in turn brought his brother Peter (John 1:41, 42). The next day Jesus found Philip on His way to Galilee, and Philip found Nathaniel (John 1:43-51). There is no evidence of haste in the selection of these disciples; just determination. James, the brother of John, is not mentioned as one of the group until the four fishermen are recalled several months later by the Sea of Galilee (Mark 1:19; Matt. 4:21). Shortly afterward Matthew is bidden to follow the Master as Jesus passed through Capernaum (Mark 2:13, 14; Matt. 9:9; Luke 5:27, 28). The particulars surrounding the call of the other disciples are not recorded in the Gospels, but it is believed that they all occurred in the first year of the Lord's ministry.

As one might expect, these early efforts at soul winning had little or no immediate effect upon the religious life of His day, but that did not matter greatly. For as it turned out these few early converts of the Lord were destined to become the leaders of His church that was to go with the Gospel to the whole world, and from the standpoint of His ultimate purpose, the significance of their lives would be felt throughout eternity. That's the only thing that counts.

What is more revealing about these men is that at first they do not impress us as being key men. None of them occupied prominent places in the Synagogue, nor did any of them belong to the Levitical priesthood. For the most part they were common laboring men, probably having no professional training beyond the rudiments of knowledge necessary for their vocation. Perhaps a few of them came from families of some considerable means, such as the sons of Zebedee, but none of them could have been considered wealthy. They had no academic degrees in the arts and philosophies of their day. Like their Master, their formal education likely consisted only of the Synagogue schools. Most of them were raised in the poor section of the country around Galilee. Apparently the only one of the twelve who came from the more refined region of Judea was Judas Iscariot. By any standard of sophisticated culture then and now they would surely be considered as a rather ragged aggregation of souls. One might wonder how Jesus could ever use them. They were impulsive, temperamental, easily offended, and had all the prejudices of their environment. In short, these men selected by the Lord to be His assistants represented an average cross-section of the lot of society in their day—not the kind of group one would expect to win the world for Christ!

Yet Jesus saw in these simple men the potential of leadership for the Kingdom. They were indeed "unlearned and ignorant" according to the world's standard (Acts 4:13), but they were teachable. Though often mistaken in their judgments and slow to comprehend spiritual things, they were honest men, willing to confess their need. Their mannerisms may have been awkward and their abilities limited, but with the exception of the traitor, their hearts were big. What is perhaps most significant about them was their sincere yearning for God and the realities of His life. The superficiality of the religious life about them had not obsessed their hope for the Messiah (John 1:41, 45, 49; 6:69). They were fed up with the hypocrisy of the ruling aristocracy. Some of them had already joined the revival movement of John the Baptist (John 1:35). These men were looking for someone to lead them in the way of salvation. Such men, pliable in the hands of the Master, could be molded into a new image—Jesus can use anyone who wants to be used.

Now read chapter 1 of *How to Be a People Helper*. As you read, try to be alert to how the conclusions in this chapter can have an influence on your effectiveness as a people helper.

PERSONAL EXERCISES

If being a disciple of Jesus Christ is a basic requirement for Christian people helpers, then we need to take a look at ourselves (our values, our goals, our priorities, and our purposes in life) to see if we are making progress as disciples.

1.   The place to start this self-look is with our spiritual lives. Have you invited Christ to be

Lord and Savior of your life (John 3:16; Romans 10:9)? _____ .

Are you seeking to turn away from sin and confessing sin when it does occur (1 John 2:1; 1:9)?.
Are you regularly reading the Bible and spending time in prayer (2 Timothy 3:14-17; 1 Thessalonians 5:17)?_____ .

If you answered no to any of these questions, how do you plan to change?_____

_____ .

Remember, God doesn't leave us on our own in these areas. His Holy Spirit is both available and able to help (Galatians 5:16; John 14:26). By growing in these spiritual areas we are also growing as people helpers.

2. Look now at the page titled "Wants Me to Be." On the line in each of the squares write in the name of a significant person or persons in your life (e.g., parents, spouse, children, employer, teacher/professor, close friend, neighbor, etc.). Now list one or two things that each of these persons expects of you. What do they "want me to be" (e.g., friendly, successful, at home all the time, less critical, etc.)?

Now look at the box labeled "S". This stands for self. What expectations do you have for yourself? Write these down.

In the remaining box write the word "God." What does He "want me to be"?

When you have finished filling in the boxes, take a look at what you have written. Do you see conflicts? For example, do you want to be a disciple while your best friends want you to be less religious? Is there a disagreement between what you want and what you think God wants? In the following spaces, note any such conflicts.

_____

_____

_____

_____

_____

_____

What can you do to resolve these conflicts?

_____

_____

_____

_____

_____

_____

3. Now let's get back to the priorities in life that we mentioned earlier. What are the most important things in your life right now (e.g., getting married, making money, getting free of debt, passing a course, etc.)?

O   D

_____   _____   _____

_____   _____   _____

_____   _____   _____

_ _ _ _

S _ _ _ _

WANTS ME

TO

BE

O   D

Go back over the list, and, in the column labeled O, order this list in terms of priority. That is, the most important thing in your life should be labeled 1, the second most important should be labeled 2, etc.

Now go over the list one more time. In the column labeled D, number the *desired* order of priorities—what you really want to be most important in your life should be labeled 1, etc. Are there priorities that are not on the list but should be? If so, add these to the list and include them in the numbering.

How can you change your life in order to make it reflect the priorities listed in column D?

_____

_____

_____

_____

_____

_____

MEETING TOGETHER

If the group is large, you might begin by reminding each other of first names. In the first half of today's meeting we will be dividing into smaller groups. Ideally you should divide into groups of three. If this is not possible, divide into groups of four. When you have divided the group, sit with the other members of the group while you listen to the tape (nine minutes).

_____ ?

_____ ?

_____ ?

As indicated on the tape, share with the people in your group what you wrote in the section labeled "Personal Exercises." After about twenty minutes, the leader should call the group together for discussion of some of the following questions.

DISCUSSION QUESTIONS

1. How did you respond to the idea of sharing something about yourself with others in your smaller group? Do you think this gives you a sense of how counselees might feel? Jesus discipled people in small groups. Could your little groups of three or four be a basis for growing as disciples?

2. Do you think that the Great Commission really has anything to do with people helping, as the author implies? Give reasons for your answer.

3. In *How to Be a People Helper*, the author suggests that "a striving for personal possessions and the adherence to a secular life-style can hinder our effectiveness in obeying Christ's Great Commission." Do you agree? Can you think of some examples? How should this affect our own life-style and priorities?

WHERE DO WE GO FROM HERE?

When you leave the group, look back over the personal exercise part of this chapter. Based on your group discussion, do you want to make any changes in your priorities or way of living? If so, determine in specific ways how you will do this.

EXTRA ASSIGNMENT

If you want to learn more about discipleship, read the excellent little paperback by Robert C. Coleman, *The Master Plan of Evangelism* (Old Tappan, New Jersey: Fleming H. Revell, 1963). You might also want to look at J. Dwight Pentecost's book, *Design for Discipleship* (Grand Rapids: Zondervan, 1971).

3
WHAT KIND OF PERSON ARE YOU?

While living in Switzerland several years ago, I came across an interesting little book about the life and work of John Calvin, the reformer and theologian. Calvin had spent most of his adult life in Geneva, and it was fascinating to visit his church and other historical places that were described in the book.

One afternoon I glanced at the little volume as it lay on the coffee table in our apartment and was suddenly struck with the significance of the book's title. It was called *The Man God Mastered*. "Will anyone be saying that about me after I'm dead?" I wondered. And how does one become a person whom God masters?

These are more than theoretical questions. If we become people who are mastered by God, then our lives are likely to show these very characteristics which, according to psychological research, make us into effective people helpers. In this unit, therefore, we will look at ourselves as people who can be mastered by God, and we will make a start at people helping.

GETTING STARTED BY LOOKING TO THE BIBLE

Let's begin with one of the questions that was raised in the above paragraphs. How do we become people whom God masters? Second Peter gives us a good start in finding an answer. Please read verses 1 to 11 of 2 Peter chapter 1.

To whom is this chapter written (see verse 1)? _____

Based on your answer, what is a basic requirement for being a man or woman of God?

_____

_____

Have you committed your life to Jesus Christ and received Him into your life? _____

_____

What are the characteristics of a person who is mastered by God (see verses 5-7)?

_____   _____

23

_____   _____

_____   _____

_____   _____

Can you think of some other characteristics that might be added to the list? Try to give Biblical references.

                                                     Bible References

_____ (   )

_____ (   )

_____ (   )

_____ (   )

_____ (   )

Now let's consider how we get these characteristics. In verse 3 we see that God gives us everything that we need for a godly life. But what are we to do to develop these gifts (see verse 10)?

_____

_____

Assuming that we receive these gifts and develop them diligently, what earthly benefits can we expect? Notice that there are present earthly benefits and an eternal heavenly benefit. Make a list of these.

Earthly Benefits   *Heavenly Benefit*

verse 4   _____   verse 11   _____

verse 4   _____

verse 8   _____

verse 10 _____

Peter was a man whom God mastered. He was writing a short time before his death (verse 14), and he knew the earthly and heavenly benefits of being mastered by God. His final words in 2 Peter 3:17, 18 are a good reminder to us all.

READING

Read the following excerpt from Lawrence R. Brammer's excellent little book *The Helping Relationship.**

There is a general dictum among people helpers that says that if I want to become more effective I must begin with myself. The reason is that our personalities are the principal tools of the helping process. Combs (1969) used the term "self as instrument" in the Florida studies. This phrase means that our principal helping tool is ourselves acting spontaneously in response to the

---

* Lawrence R. Brammer, *The Helping Relationship* (Englewood Cliffs, New Jersey: Prentice-Hall, 1973), pp. 21-28. Used by permission.

rapidly changing interpersonal demands of the helping relationship. A teacher must react to new stimuli instantly, for example, with little or no thought ahead of time. How the teacher reacts is a function of who he is at that moment and how he sees his relationship with that particular student. We are behavior models for helpees no matter how we construe our helping role. They imitate our behaviors, identify with our views, and absorb our values. Although we may try to be an impartial and objective helper, the facts indicate that we cannot be such and still remain involved in the relationship. The following helper characteristics determine the nature of this relationship.

1. Awareness of self and values. There is universal agreement among practitioners and writers that helpers need a broad awareness of their own value positions. They must be able to answer very clearly the questions "Who am I?" and "What is important to me?" The reason is that this awareness assists the helper to be honest not only with himself but also with the helpee. He can say clearly, "This is where I'm at." This awareness also helps the helper to avoid unwarranted or unethical use of the helpee for his own need satisfactions. As I indicated in chapter 1, the relationship is a process of mutual need fulfillment, but the helper must know the limits of using the helping relationship for fulfilling his own psychological needs. Self-awareness provides some insurance, furthermore, against the tendency to project values to others. In every human relationship there is a fantasy of the other person that makes up a large part of our image of him. This fantasy consists of our values projected to him. For example, I may perceive the helpee from a few minimal cues as a very undependable person. The question is always, "How much of this judgment is really descriptive of him and how much is myself projected to him? Am I judging him against some vague social norm?"

While we may have opinions about traits of people we like and want to associate with, one characteristic of the effective helper is that he tries to suspend judgments of others. Although it may be helpful sometimes to confront helpees with our opinions, we should try to be descriptive of specific behaviors and to avoid labels, mainly because so frequently they are projections of our own social values.

There are numerous helping situations that test the helper's values. If a helpee is describing a sexual behavior which the helper finds unacceptable to himself, or if the helpee is talking about divorce and the helper has strong convictions about the inviolability of marriage contracts, how does the helper behave? Can he maintain his own values and still accept the helpee? Can he empathize with the helpee, yet be keenly aware of his own values as a helper and his tendencies to project and judge?

How does the helper acquire the kind of awareness described above? Obtaining counseling for himself or participating in awareness groups are key sources of self-awareness. Reflection and meditation are other means. Self-renewal workshops which focus on examination of values and getting in touch with one's self are becoming sources of expanded awareness and renewed vigor to continue in demanding helping relationships.

2. The helper has feelings too. From observations of helping specialists an impression may be gained that one needs to be "cool," to evidence behavior characterized by detachment from feelings. While effective helping implies awareness and control of one's feelings to prevent the projection of needs described above, we must realize that the helper also is *feeling* all the time. He feels, for example, the elation of helpee growth toward independence. Similarly, he feels disappointed when his own expectations for the helpee's growth do not develop. He feels depreciated when his overtures of help are spurned by the helpee. Knowing the reasons why helpee esteem needs require this kind of "rejecting" behavior is of some comfort, but helpers are inclined to respond with feelings of disappointment to others who do not value their efforts.

It is necessary to promote a feeling of confidence in the helper; and there seems to be a nice balance between the stance of the know-it-all expert and a self-effacing attitude such as, "I don't have any special talent or skill; I'm just little old me!" Am I aware, for example, of my tendencies to depreciate myself as a helper on the one hand, or my tendency to act like a "guru," one who has the answers, on the other? Furthermore, why do I need to create a mystique about myself that promotes awe and dependency in the helpee?

As a helper I must learn to deal effectively with my confusion and value conflicts. When are self-assertion and expression of freedom important, for example, and when are conforming and adjusting the appropriate behaviors? The helper often is caught between liberating forces of growing independence and society's need to punish deviates, force conformity, and banish rebels. The helper must learn to live with this basic human conflict in himself and his helpees.

Feelings of power over helpees come quite unexpectedly. Unless the helper is wary, he is trapped into a smug controlling feeling when the helpee expresses strong dependence on him, or when he indicates that the helper has influence over him. When a helpee expresses profuse gratitude, for example, I begin to wonder if I really provided a condition in which he felt he helped himself, or whether he felt I did it for him. The latter feeling denies his own assertive self-help. It is like a child telling his mother, with some annoyance, "I don't need you anymore!"

Professional helpers label these unconscious feelings toward helpees as "countertransference effects," meaning that the helper's needs are expressed in behaviors such as dominating, overprotecting, loving, pleasing, seducing, or manipulating helpees. These feelings are "transferred" from the helper's own past relationships with significant people to the present helpee relationship.

The only known antidotes to the kinds of behavior described above are awareness of one's particular tendencies to "transfer" his own needs, problems, and unrecognized feelings to the helpee. This awareness can be obtained primarily through feedback about one's behavior in individual and group counseling experiences. Furthermore, one needs to have his personal life in such good order that he can take disappointment, frustration, demanding confrontations, and intensive encounters in helping relationships without projecting them to helpees, or developing personal symptoms such as depression, withdrawal, or physical complaints. As a helper one needs a strong "ego," meaning confidence in one's own worth as a person. Again, protections against self-defeating conditions are a counseling relationship for one's self occasionally and a satisfying personal life to provide continuous self-renewal. Helping is an emotionally demanding activity, even when done informally, and some provisions must be made for the helper to "recharge his own battery" occasionally.

3. Helper as model. The helper functions as a model to the helpee in the relationship whether he wants to or not. There is considerable support in the research literature for the power of models for acquiring socially adaptive as well as maladaptive behaviors (Sarason and Ganzer 1971). It is more controversial, however, whether a helper also must be a model of decorum, maturity, and effectiveness in his personal life. I have two reactions on this issue. The first is that

the helper must have a fulfilling life himself, or he will tend to use the helping relationship too much for satisfaction of his own unmet needs. The second reaction is that the helper's credibility may be questioned if he has a chaotic personal life. If his marital life is stormy, for example, or if his children have constant brushes with police, the validity of his work is likely to be questioned.

The helper often is caught in the squeeze between his own self-fulfilling desires to deviate from local community norms and to resist pressures to conform, particularly if he is employed by local agencies such as schools and churches. Our society is reaching a point, however, where wide variations in behavior are more acceptable, and where the private life of the prospective helper is more respected. The final standard for judging the appropriateness of the helper's behavior is the helpee's judgment about the helper's usefulness in the present relationship.

Behaving like an "expert" helper in the eyes of the helpee is important to the helping relationship. Schmidt and Strong (1970) studied the behaviors seen as "expert" and "inexpert" from the helpee's viewpoint. Those helpers perceived as expert treated the student helpees as equals, with friendly, attentive behavior. They spoke with confidence and liveliness. The "expert" helpers came prepared with knowledge about the helpee, his background and reasons for coming, and they moved quickly to the heart of the problem. Those perceived as "inexpert" were tense, fearful, rambling, uncertain, or overly cool and casual, communicating disinterest and boredom. Because of their more enthusiastic responsiveness to the helpees, the less experienced and less professionally trained counselors often were perceived as the "experts" by the student observers. To have influence with helpees, then, the helper must consider how he is perceived by the helpee and what kind of model he is presenting.

4. Interest in people and social change. A vital question for the helper is "Why do I want to help?" I stated earlier that the helper has needs too and that he can expect some kinds of satisfactions to maintain his helping behaviors. It is not too productive to engage in extensive self-probings about why one wants to help, but it is necessary to have some awareness of the fact that he is acting for himself as well as for some assumed value for the helpee. It is evident, however, that the effective helper is very interested in people. In his studies of effective helpers, Combs (1969) found that a central value was their concern with people rather than things and with an altruistic stance moving outward toward helping people rather than a more narcissistic focus on themselves. The effective helpers also identified with humanity rather than seeing themselves separated from people.

If helpers are asked "Why do you help?" they are likely to come up with pious statements designed to impress others with their expansive humanity and virtue. Honest feedback from colleagues, friends, and helpers is a key source of awareness of motives for helping. Another is just to accept the probable fact that we have many basic needs and personal growth goals fulfilled by helping others. Such needs are self-worth, status, and intimacy. The standard for judging is the pleasure or pain experienced during and after a helping relationship; for example, "I just feel good about myself when I see people like Joe grow in social effectiveness." Just as some persons experience pleasure after creating a poem or playing a musical composition, so helpers experience a glow of satisfaction in experiencing human growth before their eyes and realizing that they had some part in facilitating this growth.

There appears to be a strong altruistic quality in helping types also. Granted, we could rationalize altruism quickly in terms of need theory or reward-punishment principles, but the love motive, in the Greek "agape" sense of nonerotic personal caring, is strong in helpers. They honestly feel that they are helping out of a deep love of humanity focused on a particular person. This motive has strong theological overtones and reflects the helper's profound commitment to a special view of the world and his place in it. Although I subscribe to a considerable portion of this kind of motivation for helping, I want to be sure my awareness "antennae" are tuned to feedback from the helpee so that I can check the validity of my views and the soundness of my motives. I want to know, for example, when my needs to convert others to my way of thinking and valuing, or to behave according to my model, become too strong.

It is my opinion that the Hebraic-Christian tradition has contributed in a solid way to the helping climate of our civilization. Yet, like knives, drugs, or machines, helping motives quickly can become destructive tools in the hands of naive or zealous users.

Findings from studies on altruistic behavior have some relevance here (Baron and Liebert 1971). Seeing a *model* of helping, that is, watching someone in the act of helping someone else, tends to elicit this kind of behavior in the watchers. A strong *reciprocity* principle operates in altruistic behavior also. People tend to help those from whom they have received help, since our society has a strong "give and get" norm and a subtle system of social debts and credits. There is also a social *responsibility* factor operating, since people tend to help those who are dependent upon them, even when the rewards for helping seem to be remote.

Interpersonal *attraction* was a principle operating in some of the helping studies. *Liking* the person and being of *similar background* promoted altuism. A compliance principle seemed to explain some behavior where helping was expected in order to obtain *social approval*. This is enough discussion to indicate that altruistic motives are extremely complex; and it is likely that a variety of socially conditioned as well as consciously chosen values motivate helping acts.

General helping acts often grow out of strong social support and change motives. From the standpoint of our collective self-interest, and perhaps survival as a race, it is essential that people function supportively to one another. When they do not, we are all jeopardized in the form of crime, accidents, and pollution. We must have more people concerned about the welfare of others if our society is to survive. This is the kind of condition that creates activist-helpers who are concerned primarily with changing social conditions to meet human welfare needs, rather than merely helping individuals to cope with the demands of an "ailing" society. A growing number of help-oriented people are seeing their function as change agents for large systems. Their goal is to create a people-serving and growth-facilitating society rather than to perpetuate destructive practices of present society.

5. Helper ethics. When personal beliefs about people and society become outlined clearly, they serve as conscious guidelines for action. When one values the helpee's welfare, for example, he will do nothing to harm him. If someone asks for personal information confided to him, he will not divulge it. He would regard that information as a symbol of trust.

When these ethical principles are shared widely among helpers, they become written down and codified. Professional people-helper groups have ethics codes. These codes are formal guidelines for action, and they reflect common values regarding helper-helpee relationships and responsibilities. The key value of a code to a helper is to give him some frame of reference for his own judgments about client welfare and social responsibility. For example, while his ultimate allegiance generally is to the society he serves, the helper's primary responsibility is to his helpee client. Information will not be revealed unless there is clear and imminent danger to the helpee or other people. The complexities and variations in circumstances make this topic too large for further discussion here; but hopefully it interests you sufficiently to delve into the details of ethical principles and codes among the suggested readings. The main point to emphasize here is that the helper becomes committed to a set of ethical behaviors that are reflections of his own moral standards, society's codes, and the norms of the helping professions.

6. Helper responsibility. Related to the helper's ethical behavior is the issue of how much responsibility he can assume for his own and his helpee's behavior. Responsibility is a judgmental term defined only in terms of a specific helping context; but there are common understandings about responsible helper behavior. The helper behaves ethically, as defined above, meaning that he balances helpee welfare and social expectations. He knows and respects his personal limitations, so that he does not promise unrealistic outcomes. He refers helpees to specialists when his limitations and their needs so dictate; and the helper maintains contact until the specialist takes responsibility for a new relationship.

The helper defines his relationship to the helpee in a manner clear to the helpee. There is a clear norm among professional helpers that should, in my opinion, apply to all types of helpers. This norm says that once a helping relationship is agreed upon, the helper will do all in his power to make it productive until such time as a transfer of responsibility is made to another helper, or until either person voluntarily and formally terminates the relationship.

The issue of how much responsibility a helper can or should take for a helpee's behavior is very unclear. Some helpers move to one extreme of saying that the helpee is the only one responsible for the outcomes or consequences of the relationship. Others maintain a very accountable stance under the assumption that the helper is mainly responsible for what happens to the helpee as a result of the helping relationship. It is my observation that most authorities view this issue as a shared responsibility. They keep this question open and move along the responsibility continuum according to their best judgment of the specific condition and age of the helpee. The helpee is responsible for his own decisions, for example, including how much of himself he is ready to reveal. The helper is responsible for presenting ideas, reactions, or support as deemed appropriate or as requested by the helpee.

There is a misperception about responsible behavior in regard to helpees revealing personal data about themselves. There is the common (and questionable) assumption that if the helper just listens to the helpee this can do no harm; but listening has a powerful uncovering effect on the helpee. He often pulls down his protective psychological armor while he becomes more open. The effect on the helpee is often a feeling of vulnerability and hurt, or sometimes fear over having revealed too much. Responsible helper behavior is knowing when to "cap off" these self-revelations, or expressions of feeling. One of the great dilemmas of helping is that we can't be helpful if the helpee is not open, yet the most helpful thing we might do is assist him in limiting his self-revelations.

Now read chapter 2 of *How to Be a People Helper*.

PERSONAL EXERCISES

During our first unit we stressed the importance of revealing ourselves to others and being open to what others think of us. It is unlikely, however, that you will want to reveal *everything* about yourself right now (if ever), and you might not be completely open to the opinions of others. It is important, therefore, that you think now about your characteristics or problems and decide what you would be willing to reveal in a practice counseling situation and what you might prefer to keep to yourself.

In the exercises which follow, you will be asked to list your problems and concerns in life. You alone will decide whether or not to reveal this list or parts of it to others.

Thinking about ourselves in this way helps to clarify our own problems and enables us to decide what to share when we meet later for our practice sessions.

Below are some of the kinds of problems that people have:

—I lose my temper easily and then I'm frustrated because I get mad.

—I can't get along with my parents. We're arguing all the time.

—I need to be liked by others. I seldom do anything that might offend others, lest they criticize or reject me.

—I'm sensitive and easily hurt.

—I have a very low opinion of myself. Sometimes I think I even encourage people to criticize me, and then I feel put down further.

—I'm shy and have real problems in relating to others.

—I'm lazy, especially when it comes to studying. I'm very much afraid I might flunk out.

—I'm a Christian but I never seem to get around to reading my Bible or praying.

—I'm a very critical person, so much so that other people don't want to be around me.

—I have problems with my sexual thoughts and actions. Sometimes I go too far and then I feel guilty.

—I'm always putting people down. I never seem to encourage others.

—I'm a coward. I find it hard to stand up for my rights, and then people push me around.

Now make a list of your own. Remember, this will be kept as confidential as you choose. Use more paper if you need it.

1. _____

_____

2. _____

_____

3. _____

_____

4. _____

_____

5. _____

_____

6. _____

_____

7. _____

_____

8. _____

_____

9. _____

_____

10. _____

_____

11. _____

_____

12. _____

_____

13. _____

_____

14. _____

_____

15. _____

_____

When you have completed your list, go back and mark each entry as follows:

Place an X through the numbers of those items that you don't want to discuss at all.

Place a P next to the numbers of the statements about yourself that you would be willing to discuss in a practice helping session.

Place an H in front of the statements that might influence your effectiveness as a helper.

Now go back to the P responses. Number these, assigning number 1 to the statement that you would be most willing to share and discuss, number 2 to the second most likely item for discussion, and so on.

As you think about it, you can add to the list.

MEETING TOGETHER

Listen first to the tape (nine minutes). Following the tape, two chairs should be placed in the center of the circle facing each other. One volunteer should play the role of helper and the other of helpee, and the remainder of the group will serve as observer-evaluators. Use the Role Play Rating Scale (see page 109) to record your observations. Stop after about ten or fifteen minutes and discuss the following questions:

1. How did the observer-evaluators view the role-play session? What was good about it? What was not so good?

2. How did the helper and helpee evaluate the session?

3. How could role-play sessions be improved in the future?

DISCUSSION QUESTIONS

1. Can you summarize what is meant by discipleship counseling?
2. Do you think empathy, warmth, and genuineness can be learned? How?
3. How could we motivate helpees who aren't especially enthusiastic about being helped?
4. Look at the diagram on page 36 of *How to Be a People Helper.* Do you have this kind of discipling relationship with others? If not, how can you establish such relationships?

WHERE DO WE GO FROM HERE?

Think about the role play that occurred in this session. What did you learn about people helping that will improve your own practice sessions and your future work as a people helper? Keep evaluating as you go through this program.

EXTRA ASSIGNMENT

If you want to do something extra, a) you could decide to do some additional role play outside the group meetings, and b) you might read chapters 1 and 2 of Lawrence M. Brammer's *The Helping Relationship* (Englewood Cliffs, New Jersey: Prentice-Hall, 1973).

4

HOW WELL DO YOU UNDERSTAND PEOPLE?

If we really want to help people we must try to understand them. This is a basic principle of people helping. Of course we don't always succeed in our attempts to understand. Human beings are very complex creatures, and it is unlikely that any one of us can completely know another person. But our attempts to be understanding convey an attitude which the helpee quickly senses, and this speeds the helping process.

Several years ago I was given a little plaque on which was printed an Indian prayer:

> Great Spirit
> grant that I may not
> criticize my neighbor
> until I have walked a mile
> in his moccasins.

Here is one of the best ways of understanding—experiencing things from the other person's perspective (where possible) and trying to see the world from his or her point of view. In this fourth unit we will work on this ability to understand and see things through the other person's eyes.

GETTING STARTED BY LOOKING TO THE BIBLE

According to the Bible, Jesus has a perfect understanding of human needs and problems. Look, for example, at Hebrews 2:18 and 4:15, 16. What does this tell us about Jesus' ability to understand our needs?

_____

_____

_____

Now turn to Philippians chapter 4. Writing from prison, the Apostle Paul gave some general advice to members of the church at Philippi:

verse 1 _____ in the Lord

verse 2 _____ in the Lord

verse 4 _____ in the Lord

What relevance do these instructions have for us as people helpers?

_____

_____

_____

Notice next that the writer is concerned with the *feelings*, the *thoughts*, and the *actions* of his readers. As people helpers, we too must try to understand and help people in all three of these areas.

Look first at feelings. Verses 5, 6, and 7 talk about patience, freedom from anxiety, and peace. How do we help people, including ourselves, to get these?

verse 5—patience _____

verse 6—freedom from anxiety _____

verse 7—peace _____

Verse 8 deals with our thoughts. In your own words, summarize what this verse is saying.

_____

How does this tie in with your people helping? _____

_____

Verses 9-12 deal with the actions of the believer. In verse 9, what are believers supposed to do? _____

_____

Does this have any relevance to people helping? _____

_____

What had Paul learned, as reported in verses 11 and 12?_____

_____

Can people helping involve helping people to accept their circumstances? _____

Paul was probably a pretty understanding man. Why? _____

_____

Like Paul, we can learn to be more sensitive to the emotions, ideas, and behavior of others. This sensitivity will increase our people helping effectiveness.

READING

The following excerpt is taken from *Living in Peace*, written by the author several years ago (Wheaton, Illinois: Key Publishers, 1970).

It could be argued that smooth interpersonal relations depend on our relationship to Christ and on our willingness to honestly face ourselves. By understanding—even partially—our own self-centered attitudes and prejudices, and by trying to change our behavior, we can better interact with others. When we stop trying to manipulate people selfishly and instead relate to them as individuals, they are more likely to respond favorably to us.

All of this does not hide the fact, however, that interpersonal relations involve more than one person. Other people are also involved, and in our attempts to get along we must look beyond ourselves and learn to see how others view the world.

Every once in a while, some enthusiastic football player grabs the ball in the excitement of a game and runs the wrong way. To the people in the stands, this is an act of great foolishness, but to the athlete as he runs down the field, his actions are perfectly sensible. Later, when he realizes his mistake, the football player will agree with the evaluation of the fans, but as he is running he is doing what appears to him to be most reasonable and necessary.

This example illustrates a very basic truth about human behavior. The way people act can always be seen from two perspectives: from the point of view of the observer and from the view of the actor. Very often, the person who is acting, and the people who watch, see things from different perspectives. Later, both views of the situation may change, but *at the instant of action* most people do what they think is the most rational and effective thing to do in the situation as they understand it.

If we want to understand and get along with other people we must try to see things from the other's point of view as much as possible. When we fail to accurately perceive the other person, the stage is set for interpersonal conflict. As an example, let us suppose that a young couple are out on their first date together. At the end of the evening they arrive at her doorstep, and as she thanks him for the evening, the girl smiles. To her the smile may mean, "I have enjoyed being with you." To him the smile may mean, "Why don't you kiss me goodnight?" Let us assume (and this does not take much imagination) that the young man acts in accordance with *his* perception and kisses the girl. She may or may not be pleased about this and will act accordingly—perhaps by slapping his face, perhaps by smiling again.

On a first date, there may be misunderstanding and awkward moments because the couple does not know each other well enough. Later, when a man and a woman have been married for many years, they know each other well and can even predict how, in a given situation, the other will think and act. Because they understand each other's perceptions, the husband and wife are capable of greater understanding and smoother interpersonal relations.

This is illustrated in figure 1. In part A, we see two people, P1 and P2, viewing event X. If P1 and P2 speak the same language, have grown up in the same culture, and have had similar past experiences, they are likely to largely agree in their view of X. They see it from a similar perspective and they can readily understand the other's point of view. In part B, however, P3 and P4, perhaps because of different backgrounds or past education, see event X from very different angles. As a result, they may reach different conclusions about X and have trouble communicating.

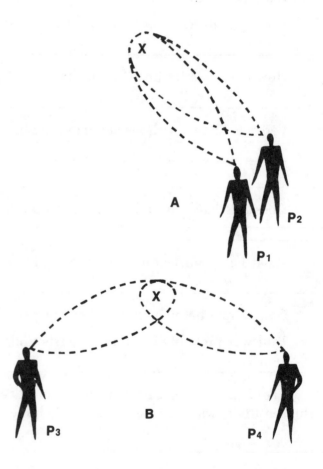

Figure 1. **Ways of Viewing Events.** Event or situation X may be viewed by two people who have similar perspectives (A) or by people whose viewpoints may differ substantially (B).

For smooth interpersonal relations and effective communication, it is not necessary that we *agree with* each other's position. On the contrary, healthy, respectful disagreement is often desirable and has probably helped man in his progress. But we must try to *see* the other person's view. We must attempt to appreciate his beliefs, values, experiences, hopes, and needs. A good place to try this is in the home or the church, where personal tensions are often present.

Before leaving this topic, it must be pointed out that individuals differ not only in their views of external objects and events, but also in their opinions about people. Figure 2 illustrates three views of person C. A has a view of C, B has view of C, and C has a set of opinions about himself. In this situation, all three agree on some things about C (see the shaded area), but there are other issues on which A and B agree but C does not. Likewise, there are views held in common only by A and C or by B and C, as well as some opinions held by each of the observers alone.

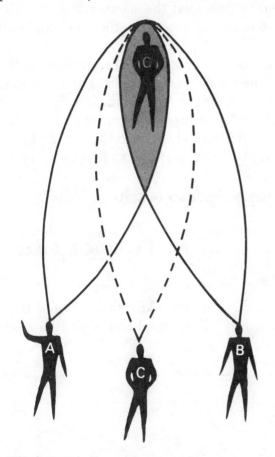

Figure 2. **Three Views of One Person.** C may be viewed from A's perspective, from B's perspective, or from the perspective of C himself. Some of these views overlap while others are unique to the viewer.

It is unlikely that two people will ever completely agree in their viewpoints, but the more information we have about an event or person, the more we can learn to appreciate and partially understand the other's point of view. Instead of arguing or concluding that the other person is blind to the facts, we should try to understand his perspective. In doing so, we must realize that others, like us, tend to see things in accordance with their personal prejudices, self-concepts, and unique past experiences.

Seeing things from another's perspective is not difficult if, like P1 and P2 of figure 1, two people have similar backgrounds and attitudes. On some issues, for example, Christians are able to get along quite well because their basic views are in agreement. The early believers never debated the existence of God, the resurrection of Christ, or the possibility of miracles because everybody accepted the truth of these and similar doctrines.

It is when people approach an issue with different viewpoints, as in the lower half of figure 1, that problems begin to arise. Even the spiritual giants in the early church had differences of opinion (that is, different perspectives) regarding the relationships between Jewish and Gentile Christians. When this happened, they met and discussed their differences so that they could eventually arrive at a mutual understanding and resolution of the difficulties (Acts 11:1-18; 15:1-31).

The ability to appreciate another's perspective is not an inborn characteristic, nor is it a gift which is bestowed when we become Christians. It is, instead, a skill which is constantly to be learned and perfected. Many people have the false opinion that psychologists can read minds and that they are always analyzing others, even at social gatherings. Most professional counselors have at some time seen people laugh nervously and politely excuse themselves from the presence of the supposed mindreader. While no psychologist has such powers (and it probably would not be good if they did) most counselors *have* become highly skilled and astute in their ability to observe human behavior. The professional counselor has learned through his training and experience to watch people carefully and to appreciate what their behavior means. But this ability is not limited to a few specialists. All of us can increase our skills in this area by observing people and by trying to think and feel as they do. If the checkout girl in the supermarket is a little grouchy at five o'clock, put yourself in her shoes and think how you would feel after standing in one spot all day pounding a cash register and handing out green stamps. By understanding her situation, we are better able to appreciate the tired frustration which she may feel, and we can better tolerate her grouchiness.

In all of this we must remember that our understanding will never be perfect. We can see things "as if" we were another person, but we can never completely get into his skin and think from his perspective. Only God can do that. He understands perfectly because He perceives with such accuracy (I Samuel 16:7). Jesus demonstrated repeatedly that He could see people as they really were, even though He did not always like what He saw. He did not, for example, approve of the motives of the religious leaders who tried to trick Him with their questions, but He understood nevertheless —

just as He does today.

As we learn to be more perceptive, we who are Christians have the guidance and teaching of the Holy Spirit. Paul acknowledged this in his prayer for the Colossians. "We are asking God," he stated, "that you may see things . . . from his point of view by being given spiritual insight and understanding" (Colossians 1:9). Our little minds can only partially comprehend the viewpoint of God (Romans 11:33), but this helps us to more accurately see others.

To improve our relationships with others we must seek the guidance of the Holy Spirit as we actively work to see objects, events, situations, and persons (including ourselves) through the other person's eyes.

Turn now to *How to Be a People Helper* and read chapter 3.

PERSONAL EXERCISES

Printed below are seven statements which you might hear in a discussion with someone who needs help. Read each statement and then try to summarize what the speaker feels and the content of what was said. In writing your answers try to see things from the other person's point of view. The first answer is filled in.

Please note that the purpose of this exercise is not to come up with solutions to the speaker's problems. You are not trying to "psych out" the speaker's motives or to make guesses about his or her life. Based solely on the statement that is presented, first summarize the *feeling* that is being expressed and then state in your own words what the speaker seems to be saying.

1. "I want to get a date with Bonny for next weekend but I always seem to panic when it comes time to call her. Probably if I did get a date I'd just botch it all up, so I guess I'll be by myself again this Saturday."

How does this person feel? *frustrated, inadequate, lacking in self-confidence, perhaps anxious.*

Summarize the content of what the speaker is really saying. *I'm convinced that I'm not competent in my dating situations.*

2. "My best friend just turned her back on me and I don't even know why. We've been friends for several years and now she doesn't even want to talk to me. I just can't figure out some people."

How does this person feel?

Summarize the content of what the speaker is really saying.

3. "I can't understand why anyone as young as me would get cancer. My husband is keeping up a brave front but he knows I'm dying and so do I. But we never talk about it. It's a phony, unreal situation."

How does this person feel? _____

_____

Summarize the content of what the speaker is really saying. _____

_____

4. "It's really frustrating. I mean, every time I tell a lie I get disgusted with myself and decide I'll never do it again. Then before you know it I tell another lie and get mad at myself all over again."

How does this person feel? _____

_____

Summarize the content of what the speaker is really saying. _____

_____

5. "It's none of your business how I feel or what I do with my time. I wish you'd quit playing amateur psychiatrist and mind your own business."

How does this person feel? _____

_____

Summarize the content of what the speaker is really saying. _____

_____

6. "I'm really discouraged. Nothing ever seems to go right with me. Sometimes I think I'd like to end it all."

How does this person feel? _____

_____

Summarize the content of what the speaker is really saying. _____

_____

7. "I'm looking forward to going to college. It will be a chance to get away from home and find some new friends. Of course it will mean leaving my friends here, and I'm not sure if I can find a good church there. I've never lived away from home and my teachers tell me that my course work will be harder."

How does this person feel? _____

_____

Summarize the content of what the speaker is really saying. _____

_____

The following are some responses which you might make to each of the above. Check the response which best shows an *understanding* of the helpee's situation. Remember, we are not trying to give solutions here. Our goal is to say something which lets the speaker know that we understand.

1. _____ (a) I'm sure Bonny would go out with you if you asked.

_____ (b) Why do you feel you'd botch things up?

_____ (c) It sounds like you're pretty frustrated about your whole dating activities.

_____ (d) I bet you'd like some help with your dating.

2. _____ (a) It must be very frustrating to have something like this happen, especially when you don't know why.

_____ (b) You've got a right to be mad.

_____ (c) Why don't you talk to her about the whole situation?

_____ (d) Some people are pretty hard to figure out.

3. _____ (a) But remember the Bible says that all things work together for good to them that love God.

_____ (b) Some things we just can't understand, can we?

_____ (c) Are you ready to meet your Maker? This would certainly make it easier to face death.

_____ (d) Probably it's pretty difficult for you to face death alone when you want so much to talk about it with your husband.

4. _____ (a) Sometimes it's hard to control yourself, isn't it?

_____ (b) I'm glad you realize, however, that lying is a sin. But we know from 1 John 1:9 that God forgives.

_____ (c) You'll just have to keep trying harder to stop.

_____ (d) Keep working on it and someday the problem will be gone.

5. _____ (a) Don't get mad at me, I'm only trying to be helpful.

_____ (b) You seem to be angry with me.

_____ (c) Really it is my business, since you're a fellow human being who needs help.

_____ (d) I'm sorry you're so frustrated and angry about my attempts to be helpful.

6. _____ (a) But a Christian should never consider suicide.

_____ (b) Sounds like nothing is going well with you right now.

_____ (c) I wonder if things are really as bad as you imply.

_____ (d) Cheer up! You need to develop a more positive outlook on life.

7. _____ (a) Do you want to go or don't you?

_____ (b) It must be pretty scary to think of the harder courses.

_____ (c) It sounds like you're both apprehensive and enthusiastic about going to college.

_____ (d) I wouldn't worry too much. Most freshmen feel like you do.

These responses will be discussed further when you meet as a group.

MEETING TOGETHER

The tape this week discusses "understanding," beginning with a consideration of the exercises that you did before this meeting (13½ minutes).

S _____

O _____

L _____

E _____

R _____

Following the tape, discuss the group members' answers to the above exercises. Take notes in the following space. The whole group can discuss together or you can divide into your role play groups for the discussion.

_____
_____
_____
_____
_____
_____
_____
_____
_____
_____

After about fifteen minutes, do another role play. Try to concentrate on understanding responses. If you were a helper or helpee last time, switch roles. In the back of this growthbook, on page 110, there is another Role Play Rating Scale for use this week.

DISCUSSION QUESTIONS

1. Summarize the fourth, fifth, and sixth principles of discipleship counseling, as described in _How to Be a People Helper_. Do you have any questions about these principles? Any disagreements with the author?

2. Look over the chart on listening. Which of these principles can and should be applied to your family, your work, your relationships with people at church, etc.?

3.   What is your reaction to the SOLER concept described on the tape?

4.   Look back at the diagrams which appear earlier in this chapter of the growthbook. Can you think of examples from your own experience to illustrate figures 1 and 2?

WHERE DO WE GO FROM HERE?

Try to practice seeing things from the perspective of other people, listening attentively, and developing a SOLER posture when you talk with others. These can carry over into all of your contacts with others and can improve your interpersonal relationships as well as your people helping.

EXTRA ASSIGNMENT

Read chapter 6 of Lawrence M. Brammer's book *The Helping Relationship* (Englewood Cliffs, New Jersey: Prentice-Hall, 1973), pp. 81-110. The chapter is entitled "Helping Skills for Understanding." You could also benefit from reading John W. Drakeford's *The Awesome Power of the Listening Ear* (Waco, Texas: Word, Inc., 1967).

5
WHAT IF
THE HELPEE
IS YOUR FRIEND?

Many years ago Freud, the founder of psychoanalysis, instructed his fellow psychiatrists that they should maintain a detached aloofness during counseling sessions. Some professional counselors still maintain this posture during counseling, but today most helpers try to be more down-to-earth and warm in relating to helpees.

When the person in need of help is your friend you really can't be aloof, even if you wanted to be. Perhaps one of the reasons for the effectiveness of peer counseling is that the helper and helpee have such a warm, trusting relationship with one another. In this unit we will consider the *feeling* aspect of helping, with special emphasis on helping friends.

GETTING STARTED BY LOOKING TO THE BIBLE

The Bible says a lot about helping our brothers. "Brethren" in the Scriptures is a term that applies to fellow believers, but presumably such people are especially close to us. The following are references to ways in which we can help these brethren. In each case, write a practical guideline to helping these friends.

Zechariah 7:9 _____

_____

Matthew 18:15 _____

_____

Luke 17:3, 4 _____

_____

Romans 14:10-13 _____

_____

1 Corinthians 8:9-13 _____

_____

Galatians 6:1 _____

_____

James 1:19 _____

_____

James 2:1-5 _____

_____

James 5:19, 20 _____

_____

1 John 2:9, 10; 1 Thessalonians 4:9; Hebrews 13:1 _____

_____

Can you think of other Bible passages that deal with brotherly people helping? List some of these below, indicating the practical guidelines that each contains.

_____ __:__ _____

_____ __:__ _____

_____ __:__ _____

_____ __:__ _____

_____ __:__ _____

READING

Read chapter 4 of *How to Be a People Helper*.

The following excerpt is taken from the author's book *Effective Counseling* (Carol Stream, Illinois: Creation House, 1972), pp. 13-39. This was written to help pastoral counselors with their work, but many of the same principles apply to lay people helpers working with their friends.

Counseling can be defined as a relationship between two or more persons in which one person (the counselor) seeks to advise, encourage and/or assist another person or persons (the counselee[s]) to deal more effectively with the problems of life. Counseling may have any number of goals, including a changing of the counselee's behavior, attitudes or values; preventing more serious problems from developing; teaching social skills; encouraging expression of emotions; giving support in times of need; instilling insight; guiding as a decision is made; teaching responsibility; stimulating spiritual growth; and helping the counselee to

mobilize his inner resources in times of crisis. Unlike psychotherapy, counseling rarely aims to radically alter or remold the personality.

Because of his position, the church leader is in a unique counseling position. Unlike the professional, the lay counselor is often well-acquainted with the counselee's personal, home, and community background. The church leader can visit in homes, he is often a trusted friend, and he is available—as near as the church or telephone. In addition, the Christian counselor freely makes use of spiritual resources such as prayer and Bible reading. Since he strives to be an "expert in spiritual growth," the Christian counselor can be of special help to people who are concerned about God, values, sin, forgiveness, guilt, and other religious questions....

Good counseling is difficult work. It is time-consuming, emotionally draining, physically exhausting, and frequently unsuccessful. By developing proficiency in the following skills and techniques, however, we should be able to increase our overall counseling effectiveness.

BEFORE THE INTERVIEW

Whenever possible, it is best to spend a few minutes in preparation prior to the start of a counseling session. When we receive guests into our homes, we usually tidy the house and give the appearance that the guest is welcome and expected. A person coming for counseling should be received with at least as much courtesy. If he feels that he is "taking the valuable time of a busy man" he may feel guilty, rushed, and hence unable to communicate. It is a good procedure, therefore, to straighten the papers on the desk, get the room in readiness, and arrange to keep the counseling period free from interruptions.

Then we should review the counselee's case history and remind ourselves of the details of any previous counseling with him. It is embarrassing to get one person's problem confused with another's, and it is distressing to the counselee, who naturally prefers to think that he and his problems are uppermost in your mind.

For the Christian counselor it is also important to prepare for the interview with prayer. We can commit the counseling session to God, asking that we will be made sensitive to the needs and feelings of the counselee, and that we will be led by the Holy Spirit as we counsel. Such prayer is no substitute for training and preparation, but all our activities, including those for which we are highly trained, should be committed to the Lord, who guides our thoughts and actions (Prov. 16:3; 3:5-6). The counselor should meet the counselee at the exact time of the appointment. Being ten or fifteen minutes late and giving no real explanation will make the counselee assume he has been forgotten or that he isn't important enough to meet on time.

DURING THE INTERVIEW

When we meet somebody in a social situation, we do not usually engage in frantic activity to remember all the social graces our parents taught us. If the home training was adequate, the social skills appear automatically. To some extent, the same is true of counseling, for we do not "pull out a bag of tricks" as soon as a counselee enters the office. If we are aware of the following skills and think about them frequently as we prepare for counseling, many will appear automatically when we are face-to-face with the counselee. This does not mean that the counselor should not think about techniques during the interview. He should be asking himself constantly, "What is happening now?" "What am I doing?" "What is best to do next?" But the counseling session must be primarily a relationship between concerned people rather than a period during which the counselor is so concerned about skills that he forgets everything else.

Start by working on the relationship. Counselees often approach an interview with fear, trembling, and a number of misconceptions. They may be uncomfortable at the thought of discussing their personal problems and uncertain about what is going to happen during the interview. At the beginning, therefore, the counselor has a responsibility to support and stimulate the counselee. *Support* involves "breaking the ice" with a casual comment or two and inviting the counselee to have a seat. With some counselees it might be desirable to give an indication of what will happen during the interview. For example, the counselor might say, "I'm glad for this opportunity to chat about the things that are concerning you." This is much less threatening than an emotionally loaded statement like "I'm glad for this chance to counsel you about your problems."

When someone brings a problem to a psychologist, the initial contact is usually a meeting between two strangers; but in pastoral counseling, the counselor and counselee often know each other at least casually. If the counselor is a minister, he has been observed in the pulpit or met as he shakes hands at the door following the service. The Sunday school teacher or youth leader who is asked for counsel has probably demonstrated his warmth and concern for people in noncounseling situations such as Bible-study classes. These casual precounseling experiences do a great deal to establish a relationship long before the counselee ever knocks at your door.

In addition to giving support and helping the person feel more at ease, we must *stimulate* him to talk. For some counselees this is no problem because they talk freely when given the chance. But, for others, talking is difficult, even if they have requested an appointment and really want to discuss some problem. If the counselee has come voluntarily, a comment such as "What would you like to talk about today?" or "Now, you wanted to talk to me?" can get things started. Very often the counselee will respond by saying, "I just don't know where to start." At such times it might be good to show understanding: "Probably a lot of things all tie in together," and then to encourage the person: "Start anyplace and eventually we will get the whole picture," or "Begin where it seems easiest." These statements, of course, are merely examples of any number of appropriate comments.

Occasionally a person wants to talk about some problem but is reluctant to mention it. Every college counseling center has students who come requesting information for a term paper that they are writing on homosexuality, masturbation, or some similar topic; or they request help for a "friend" who has some problem. While these may be the real reasons for their coming, at times the "paper" or "friend" is a cover which enables the counselee to size up a counselor who, he hopes, will give him an opportunity to discuss his own homosexual tendencies, masturbation problems, or other concerns. A tactful suggestion that the problem may be personal will sometimes bring denials, but often this will give the counselee the encouragement he needs to start talking.

Sometimes a church leader may take the initiative by approaching a person who appears to need counseling. In such cases it is a good idea to get to your point as soon as possible. "I have missed you in church for the past several Sundays" or "I wanted to chat with you about the youth group" lets the counselee know right at the start why the interview has been requested.

Listen attentively. Church leaders spend a lot of their time talking. This, after all, is an important part of their job, but too often it carries over into interviews as the counselor feels that he must be constantly giving sage advice or asking a lot of questions. Such an attitude greatly hinders good counseling.

When we learn to listen, the counselee has the opportunity to express his feelings, "let off steam," or "get things off his chest." In so doing, he often feels better and at the same time gives us valuable information that we might have missed otherwise.

Listening is not a passive activity; it is an art which requires alert concentration and undivided attention. It has been estimated that we speak about 125 words per minute, but that our thinking is four times that fast. Therefore, it is possible to listen to a speaker and still be able to think about other things. In a counseling session we must be careful not to let our minds wander, especially when we are bored. Instead, we must listen to what is being said, try not to show disapproval or shock, and attempt to understand things from the speaker's point of view. An oc-

casional head nod, smile, "uh-huh," or general type of question (such as "What then?" "How did you feel about that?" or "Anything else?") can keep the counselee talking.

Watch carefully. A good counselor can learn a great deal by carefully observing the counselee's speech and actions. Suppose, for example, that there are changes in voice pitch and volume or shifts in the topic of conversation. If we review what was said both before and after these changes, we may detect a topic which is of special importance or concern to the counselee. Sometimes we see inconsistencies or gaps in a story. The person who says he is happy in his work but later talks about changing jobs, or the person who describes his family but forgets to mention his father, may be revealing something that we might ask about later.

The opening statement can also be revealing. "My mother sent me" gives a clue that the counselee may be somewhat less than enthusiastic about talking with a counselor. Likewise, the closing remarks often give an indication of the counselee's view of what happened. Finally, we should watch for repeated references to the same topic, for this may give a clue to what is uppermost on the person's mind.

There is an old saying that "actions speak louder than words," and this is true in many counseling situations. Tears or near-tears, fighting, shifts in posture, or changes in breathing can all be clues that the person is dealing with important emotional issues. If a student changes his position and gets a little misty-eyed when talking about grades, this may be a subject about which he is especially concerned. Sometimes it is a good idea to make a mental note about your observation and at a later time bring the topic up again. If the tears return, this is a clue that here is a potential problem, even though the student may not have identified it as such.

At this point someone may ask, "Why do all this detective work? Why don't we just deal with the guy's problem?" This would be ideal if every counselee first had an understanding of what his real problem was and, second, if every counselee were willing and able to share his problem. Very frequently, however, neither of these conditions exists. When a patient has a recurring pain, the doctor doesn't prescribe more pain pills and go on to the next patient. Instead, the physician tries to discover and treat the cause of the pain. Similarly, the counselor and counselee must work together to reach the underlying cause of the problem. When this is not clearly apparent, the counselor must be alert to the more subtle clues that the counselee is giving (usually unconsciously).

Don't be afraid of silence. When nothing is being said, most of us feel very uncomfortable; but in counseling such silence is often very meaningful. It may indicate that the counselee is struggling to control an emotion, thinking about an important issue, or debating whether to tell you more. At such times an understanding comment like "It's hard to talk sometimes, isn't it?" or an encouraging remark such as "Take your time" can let the counselee know that it is all right to be silent. The counselor can then keep quiet for a while until his counselee is ready to share more of his ideas and feelings.

Question wisely. Beginning counselors often make the mistake of asking too many questions. Once you start this, the counselee draws two kinds of conclusions. First, he concludes that counseling is simply the answering of questions that are asked by the counselor. Second, he expects that once the counselor has asked all of his questions and obtained the answers, then he will give his solution to the problem. This puts the counselor in a very awkward situation. Usually he doesn't have a "pat" solution, and sometimes he becomes so busy thinking up new questions to ask that he has no time to listen to the counselee's answers. It is best to use questions sparingly and to think before you ask.

It is probably true that "no more effective method has ever been devised for helping people reach the goals of self-knowledge and personal integration than through a profound understanding of the technique of asking questions." Jesus used questions skillfully, and the pastoral counselor would be wise to do the same.

Learn how to respond. Porter has suggested that there are five commonly used counselor responses: evaluative, interpretative, supportive, probing, and understanding. *Probing* responses are used when more information is needed or when the counselor wants to stimulate further discussion. With *understanding* responses, the counselor wants to convey his comprehension and empathy. By using *supportive* comments, the counselor tries to reassure or encourage the counselee. *Interpretative* responses are meant to teach the counselee or show him what is happening, while *evaluative* responses indicate what the counselor thinks about the goodness, rightness or wisdom of an action or idea. To this we might add *action* responses, in which the counselor tries to encourage or stimulate the counselee to engage in some kind of action . . . .

Make use of spiritual resources. Two of the greatest weaknesses of pastoral counselors are an overuse and underuse of spiritual resources. Some Christians are of the opinion that reading the Bible or saying a prayer is all that is needed for successful counseling. Sometimes this *is* all that is needed, but in most cases such an approach is likely to be unsuccessful and frustrating to the counselee. It also gives the impression that Bible reading and prayer are magic charms that suddenly make everything right. At the other extreme are pastoral counselors who tend to ignore prayer and the Scriptures in their counseling, using psychological techniques almost exclusively.

Once again, no hard and fast rules can be given for the use of prayer or Bible reading. Many Christian counselors pray aloud at the beginning and/or end of an interview, and sometimes they "feel led" to pray at other times. Paul Tournier, the famous Swiss counselor, likes to have a period of "quiet communion" during which both parties silently acknowledge the presence and influence of God. When it seems relevant, the counselor may also want to read a Bible passage during an interview. Narramore feels this makes more of an impression if the Bible is handed to the counselee and he is asked to read the indicated portion. For this, a modern-language version may be especially helpful and, whatever the translation, it is usually wise to discuss the meaning of a passage after it is read. Christian counselees should also be encouraged to spend daily time in Bible reading, prayer, and quiet meditation. It is also helpful to suggest devotional reading at times, or—when consistent with one's denominational practices—to even have a small communion service.

The extent to which spiritual resources will be used in counseling depends on the counselor, the counselees, and the problem. The Christian counselor should pray both during a personal daily time of devotions and during the day as he goes about his activities. Certainly the counselor who never prays in private will be awkward and uncomfortable if he prays in an interview. In like manner, the Christian should be thoroughly familiar with the Word of God (2 Tim. 2:15), or he won't have much success using the Bible in an interview.

For some counselees, prayer and Scripture reading during an interview will be a strengthening and reassuring experience. For others, this would be a source of considerable embarrassment and discomfort. Therefore, the counselor must use careful judgment in deciding if, when, and how he introduces such practices. To some extent, this will be dictated by the counselee's problem. The grief-stricken widow could be greatly comforted by a dependence on such spiritual resources, whereas the college student who is in danger of flunking out of school might prefer to have a short prayer followed by a long discussion of his study habits.

End positively. It is desirable to end an interview smoothly and, when possible, to have the counselee go away with feelings of hope and encouragement. But occasionally this is difficult, and counselors are sometimes at a loss to know how a counseling session should be stopped.

If things are moving smoothly, it is wise to give the counselee a hint that the end is near. By keeping a clock on the desk or on a distant wall it is possible to keep track of the time without having to keep glancing at your watch. A statement like "Our time is just about up" gives the counselee a warning but indicates that there is still time to pick up loose ends. In the remaining minutes it may be helpful to summarize what has happened during the interview, or discuss what the counselee should do next. Sometimes a word of encouragement or a short prayer is appropriate.

Occasionally counselees will bring up significant new material during these last few minutes of the interview. This may be an attempt to prolong the interview or it may indicate an unconscious desire to raise issues at a "safe" time when it is not possible to discuss the matter further. At such times a comment like "That would be a good topic for us to discuss next time" prevents the interview from continuing and gives a good opener for your next counseling session.

AFTER THE INTERVIEW

When the counselee leaves, the counselor should jot down some notes and briefly evaluate the interview. This should be done immediately so that details are not forgotten. When your reactions and a summary of the session are recorded on paper, you have a convenient "memory jogger" to consult before the next interview.

The counselor must keep the interview in his confidence. Some pastors are sincerely amazed that, even though their availability is well-advertised, still nobody comes for counseling. Frequently these are the men who like to describe counseling cases in sermons or who let counseling details slip into other casual conversations. Even when the names and details are changed, counselees and prospective counselees often decide to go for counseling to a person who will keep quiet. At times, of course, the counselor may wish to discuss the situation with a more experienced counselor for helpful suggestions, but these confidants should be few and selected with extreme care.

PERSONAL EXERCISE

In this unit we will do exercises which focus on how you might respond to helpees' statements. In each of the following, write two responses:

(a) how you would summarize the helpee's *feelings*.

(b) how you would summarize both *feeling and content* of what is being said. The first answer is completed for you. Remember, we are not to give our analysis of what is happening, our opinions, or suggested solutions. Based solely on the presented statement we are to summarize in our own words how the speaker feels, and how we would summarize his or her feelings and the content of the statement.

1. My wife and I just aren't getting along anymore. She criticizes everything I do, she's on the phone half the time yakking to her friends, and I'm beginning to think she's maybe got a boyfriend.

(a) You must feel *angry, confused and hurt* .

(b) *his wife's actions are making him think that he doesn't matter any more. This confuses him, hurts him and makes him angry.*

2. I think I must be oversexed or something. All I ever think about is sex. I want to jump in bed with every woman I see, and my mind is always thinking about how the girls I work with would look like in the nude.

(a) You must feel _____ .

(b) _____
_____ .

3.   Everything seems to be crashing down on me right now. Last week I wrecked my car, now my wife's got the flu, I've got a big exam next week, and I'm worried about our running out of money.

(a) You must feel _____ .

(b) _____
_____ .

4.   I'm really enthusiastic about being a Christian, but the Bible's so hard for me to understand. Some of the big theological words don't make sense to me and a lot of that stuff in the Old Testament is really pretty dull.

(a) You must feel _____ .

(b) _____
_____ .

5.   My dad isn't doing very well. At first he seemed to be coming out of his operation O.K., but then he developed internal bleeding and now the doctor says he's probably getting pneumonia.

(a) You must feel _____ .

(b) _____
_____ .

6.   These kids just about drive me up the wall. They're into everything. They're bawling half the time, and if one of them isn't sick, they drive me to distraction with their incessant racket.

(a) You must feel _____ .

(b) _____
_____ .

7.   I lost my job today. I'm so discouraged I could cry.

(a) You must feel _____ .

(b) _____
_____ .

MEETING TOGETHER

Let's begin today with a consideration of what you and the other group members wrote in response to the above assignment. Members of the group can read their written responses aloud and the group members can evaluate each statement. Which are the best? Why? Limit this discussion to fifteen minutes.

Now listen to the tape (eleven minutes). You might want to take notes in the space below.

_____

_____

_____

_____

_____

_____

_____

_____

Following the tape, divide up into role-play groups again. Remember the suggestions on the tape. Once again everyone should change roles from last time. As you go through this growthbook, make sure that everyone serves at least twice as helper, twice as helpee, and twice as observer-evaluator. A Role Play Rating Scale for this exercise appears on page 111.

DISCUSSION QUESTIONS

1.   Do you think you have a special gift as a counselor? Give reasons for your answer. If the answer is no, can you still be a people helper?

2.   *How to Be a People Helper* discusses the training of peer counselors. You are now almost halfway through this growthbook. How would you evaluate your training thus far? How can you make it better?

3.   Have you been guilty of excessive curiosity, confidence leaks, or an under- or overemphasis on the spiritual? How can you prevent this in the future?

4.   If lay helpers are so effective, why does the author state that "we must teach peer counselors when and how to make referrals"?

WHERE DO WE GO FROM HERE?

This is a good time to think about your own potential as a people helper. Are you improving in your skills? If so, why? If not, why not? Try to take what you learn from this growthbook and apply it to real-life helping situations.

EXTRA ASSIGNMENT

There can be real value in doing extra role plays. If the members of your role-play groups are not interested in some extra sessions, perhaps there are people in other groups who would be willing to team up for some extra sessions.

If you want to do some more reading, look at *Love Therapy*, by Paul D. Morris (Wheaton, Illinois: Tyndale House, 1974). It's a simple book but you might find it helpful.

6
WHAT DO YOU DO IN AN EMERGENCY?

Some of our most difficult challenges as people helpers come when others are in the midst of an emergency. The sudden sickness of a loved one, a serious accident, a family death—these are among the crises of life which demand instant action from sympathetic neighbors and friends. In one sense it is difficult to prepare for crises, especially those which come suddenly. Nevertheless, it is possible to get prior understanding of how people react to crises and to learn how we can be of greatest help to others in the midst of emergencies. This will be our major emphasis in this unit.

GETTING STARTED BY LOOKING TO THE BIBLE

A number of crisis situations are recorded in the Bible. Moses and the Israelites fleeing ahead of Pharoah's Egyptian armies, Jonah in the fish's belly, Daniel in the den of lions, Mary and Martha grieving over their dead brother, Jesus in Gethsemane—these are among the most familiar Biblical crises. In 2 Corinthians 11:23-28 Paul gives a list of the crises that he faced as a Christian, while the Book of Acts records a variety of emergency situations that the early believers faced.

Job was one man who experienced a series of crises, most of which appear to have occurred within a relatively short period of time. Please turn to the Book of Job and read the first two chapters.

Job, as these chapters clearly show, was a morally upright and godly man (1:1), the father of a large family (1:2), a wealthy and successful businessman, and one who enjoyed considerable prestige and status (1:3). But then a series of crises came into Job's life. Note what happened to Job's

wealth and possessions (1:14-17) _____

family (1:18, 19) _____

health (2:7) _____

_____

marriage (2:9, 10) _____

_____

status and prestige (2:11-13) _____

_____

The three men who came to help Job (see 2:11) got off to a good start. Summarize what they did as recorded in the last three verses of chapter 2.

_____

_____

Why do you think this might have been helpful to Job? _____

_____

_____

Beginning with chapter 4, however, the three men start talking. They criticize Job, accuse him of sinfulness, preach at him, and show themselves to be more of a hindrance than a help. Notice how Job reacts and how God responds.

Job 19:1-3 _____

Job 32:3 _____

Job 42:7 _____

What does all of this teach us about crisis intervention? Based on Job's experiences, make a list of do's and don'ts for helping people in crises. These lists will be discussed when you meet with your groups.

_____	_____
_____	_____
_____	_____
_____	_____
_____	_____

READING

Read chapter 5 of *How to Be a People Helper*.

Many of the crises of life concern the family. In the following article, the author of this book gives some general guidelines for helping people cope with family crises.

At first Mrs. Marshall thought it was part of a dream, but as the knocking persisted she aroused herself from a deep sleep and groped through the early morning darkness toward the door of the apartment. As she looked out into the hall the light was almost blinding, but the news conveyed by the two uniformed figures quickly shook the young seminary student's wife into a state of alertness. Her husband, on the way to an early-morning job, had been struck by a speeding car fleeing from the police. Mrs. Marshall, 24 years of age, mother of two little girls, had just discovered that she was a widow.

In every family, even in the best Christian families, there are times of stress. A woman has a miscarriage, a teenage son is arrested on a drug charge, a relative undergoes serious surgery, or a loved one—like Mrs. Marshall's husband—suddenly dies. Immediately the routines of family life are disrupted. Vacation plans are changed or abandoned. Tension and uncertainty about the future puts the family members under a strain which may persist for weeks or even months.

Unexpected or unpleasant events such as these are not the only cause of family stress. A daughter having trouble in school, a son going to college for the first time, a young couple adjusting to the first weeks of parenthood, a father learning to live in retirement—each of these events can produce anxiety tension and put strain on the family members. Even desirable events, like the start of a long-awaited vacation or the moving to a new house, pressure family members and disrupt normal routines.

How do families and family members cope with these crises? Sometimes the husband and wife start bickering, the children get on people's nerves and always seem to be arguing, everybody feels tired or drained, and we find our devotional life slipping. But there are more efficient ways than these to deal with stress in the family.

Several years ago a team of researchers from Harvard University did a study of family crises and concluded that how we cope is not necessarily determined by our character or inner strength. What is most important in times of crises is the kind of help that we get from other people.

Jesus never expected us to bear our burdens alone. He invited us to come in times of distress and give the problem to Him (Matthew 11:28-30). Like the psalmist of old, we can cast our burdens upon the Lord, knowing that He will sustain us (Psalm 55:22). Most Christians remember these comforting verses in times of stress, but very often we forget that the Word of

God also instructs us to bear one another's burdens (Galatians 6:2), to sustain each other, and to give help in time of need. When crises arise in our own families or in the families of others, there are practical things that each of us can do to help.

First, we can pray. This is not an exercise in futility or a talking to oneself. God hears our prayers of intercession for others and assures us that the effective fervent prayer of a righteous man (or family) can, in fact, change things (James 5:16).

Then, we can be available and ready to listen. Several years ago a young father whom I know discovered that he had terminal cancer. Shortly before his death he described some of the visitors who had come to his hospital room. "Some came to preach," he said, "with their three points all lined up and with all the answers. They were no help! I preferred the visitors who could listen to me or just sit there and could lay hold of God in confidence. When you are in trouble what you need is a man or woman of God."

Very often we try to distract people from their distress. We tell them to cheer up or to "get your mind off it for a while." Usually our motives for doing this are good. We feel that distraction is better than having someone face a crisis head-on. But isn't it really better to let the person talk about it—when it started, how it happened, what it feels like to be under so much stress? Jesus, who knew the inner heart of every man, nevertheless listened to people in times of crisis. To be available, ready to listen, is a major step in helping people and families face crises.

We must recognize, of course, that some people are not willing to talk about their crises or family stresses, even when a listener is available. Some of us still have the idea that talking about a problem is an admission of weakness, though in fact it is an evidence of strength. We think that the existence of a problem is a sign of spiritual inadequacy that must be kept hidden, and we fail to recognize that all Christians have problems at times, especially those who, like Paul, are serious about following Jesus Christ. Sometimes we "don't want to bother others" with our problems, but if we are to bear one another's burdens there must be a sharing of needs.

Third, we can help the family in crisis to get a realistic perspective on their problem. Often an outsider can see a problem issue more clearly. He can help the person or family under stress to keep from expecting the worst, to decide what can and cannot be done, and to provide encouragement.

At such times two common mistakes should be avoided. First, we should not give false reassurance. We can say with certainty that the Lord knows and cares about the situation, but we cannot always be sure that the Lord will heal in a given case or that the problem will go away.

Second, we should not encourage family members to blame others or themselves for the crisis. Families often do this when they are under stress. They find a family scapegoat, perhaps in the person of a grandparent or one of the children, and everything that goes wrong gets blamed on this individual. But this only makes matters worse. Blaming is a way of avoiding the truth. It encourages us to dream about what might have been or to analyze who might have been at fault, rather than to face the problem squarely. If sin has been involved, of course it must be confessed, but to dwell on the past mistakes or on the real or assumed errors of others only increases one's misery and does little to help meet the crisis.

Finally, we can challenge the person or family under stress to take some kind of action. Even doing something minor can help us to feel better and less discouraged. Perhaps we can point to where help is available, encourage them as they make a phone call or go for counseling, or wait with them outside an operating room or in a courtroom. One way in which people avoid facing a crisis is to deny that they need help. They brush away all offers of assistance and persist in the fantasy that nothing is wrong. Sometimes they refuse to do anything about a problem situation, hoping that if they do nothing the problem will disappear. When the individual family members, instead, acknowledge that there is a need, gratefully accept the help and prayers of others, and begin to think of what can be done to resolve the crisis, then a healthy solution to the problem is on the way.

In times of family crises, most of us feel at least somewhat disorganized and sapped of energy. Here is a time when others in the body of Christ can rally around with support, encouragement, and assistance, even to the point of helping with such common tasks as mowing the lawn or doing the family laundry. Every family faces periodic crises, and at such times the family members need help. We can assist others in our own families during such times of stress and we can render assistance to the families of others. To give and accept such help is a part of being a member of the body of Christ.

PERSONAL EXERCISES

1. Every one of us has had at least some crises in life. In this exercise we will consider our own life crises and ponder how others did or did not help. In completing this chart, try to list three or four crisis situations. If you cannot think of crises in your life, reread the first four paragraphs of chapter 5 in *How to Be a People Helper*. This should remind you that crises can be of varying types and need not seem dramatic to other people.

Describe the Crisis situation	What did *you* do to help?	What did *others* do to help?	What could have been done to help but was not?	What does this teach you about helping others in crises?
1.				
2.				
3.				
4.				

When you meet in your groups, you will discuss this chart. At that time you may want to make some notes below concerning what others have learned about crisis helping.

_____
_____
_____
_____
_____
_____
_____

2.   In crisis helping we discover that the helpee is sometimes too upset to talk. It becomes important, therefore, for the helper to watch for nonverbal communication. For each of the following, try to put yourself into the helpee's position, and 1) attempt to identify what he or she might be feeling and 2) indicate how you would respond to the person (verbally and/or nonverbally).

(a)   Mary, whose infant son recently died, starts crying in the middle of a discussion about the church Christmas pageant.

(1) _____

(2) _____

(b)   In the midst of a heated argument that he is observing, John suddenly starts to laugh.

(1) _____

(2) _____

(c)   Ron, a college student, shares with you that he has done something really awful. Then he stops talking.

(1) _____

(2) _____

(d)   Without warning or expression, Sue suddenly makes a comment which changes the topic of a group's conversation.

(1) _____

(2) _____

(e)   Jan, who wanted to chat with you about a problem, begins talking quickly and without giving you an opportunity to say anything.

(1) _____

(2) _____

(f)   When you ask Gene about his marriage, he moves around in his chair, shows signs of restlessness, and suggests that "it's time for him to be going."

(1) _____

(2) _____

3.   The following exercise* is designed to provide you with an opportunity to see if you can tell the difference between messages indicating affection and messages indicating hostility. Listed below are 38 messages. In the space provided, write an A if you think the message indicates affection and an H if you think the message indicates hostility. Check your answers with the answers found on page 112 at the back of this book. Review any messages that you answered incorrectly.

_____ 1. Looks directly at the other person; gives his undivided attention.

_____ 2. Offers a cigarette, cup of coffee, or other favor.

_____ 3. Greets the other person (if at all) in a cold, formal manner (refuses to shake hands, does not use other person's name, and so on).

_____ 4. Engages in friendly humor (e.g., self-directed humor or humor facetiously directed at the other person).

_____ 5. Glares at the other person.

_____ 6. Speaks in a harsh tone of voice.

_____ 7. Uses the other person's first name.

_____ 8. Physically abuses the other person (hits, shoves).

_____ 9. Yawns or shows other signs of boredom.

_____ 10. Seems at ease; has a relaxed posture; does not appear tense or exhibit nervous mannerisms.

_____ 11. Deprecates the other person's statements, accomplishments, background, hometown, alma mater, and so forth.

_____ 12. Lays verbal traps for the other person (e.g., "Just a minute ago you said [in response to leading] . . . Now you're contradicting yourself").

_____ 13. Smiles an expression of cordiality.

_____ 14. Sits close to the other person

_____ 15. Interrupts repeatedly.

_____ 16. Leans towards the other person as an expression of interest.

_____ 17. Makes casual physical contact with the other person as an expression of affection (e.g., friendly slap on the back, rap on the arm).

_____ 18. Shows consideration for the physical comfort of the other person (e.g., takes person's coat, offers more comfortable chair, adjusts window, asks permission before smoking).

_____ 19. Sits relatively far away.

_____ 20. Reduces the other person's remarks to the absurd.

_____ 21. Confides "personal" information to the other person.

_____ 22. Attempts to "snow" the other person by using overly intellectual or otherwise unfamiliar vocabulary.

_____ 23. Makes biting, sarcastic remarks about the other person.

_____ 24. Makes encouraging, reassuring remarks to the other person.

---

* Excerpted with permission from David W. Johnson, *Reaching Out: Interpersonal Effectiveness and Self-Actualization* (Englewood Cliffs, New Jersey: Prentice-Hall, 1972).

_____ 25. Uses ad hominems (e.g., "That stupid remark is about what I would expect from someone like you.").

_____ 26. Ignores the other person (by looking away from him, looking out the window, glancing repeatedly at watch, busying self with papers on desk).

_____ 27. Praises or compliments something the other person has said or done.

_____ 28. Expresses an interest in seeing and talking again with the other person.

_____ 29. Uses the "lingo" of the other person.

_____ 30. Exhibits an open and receptive facial expression.

_____ 31. Mocks or teases the other person.

_____ 32. Extends a cordial greeting to the other person.

_____ 33. Smiles when the other person makes a humorous remark.

_____ 34. Exhibits a cold, nonreceptive facial expression (e.g., set jaw; noninvolved, blank look).

_____ 35. Talks enthusiastically about the other person's hobbies or interests.

_____ 36. States his sympathy for the other person.

_____ 37. Rebuffs or hedges when asked a "personal" question; does not risk interpersonal involvement.

_____ 38. Responds directly and openly to the other person's request to know his opinion, value, attitude, or feeling.

MEETING TOGETHER

The tape for this session has more information on crisis counseling. You may want to take notes below (fifteen minutes).

Phases of Crises

1 _____

_____

2 _____

_____

3 _____

_____

4 _____

_____

5 _____

_____

6 _____

_____

Following the tape, break up into role-play groups and discuss together the chart that you completed as part 1 of the personal exercises section of this chapter.

Now discuss your answers to part 2 of the personal exercises. Did you agree in your analyses of the helpee actions?

After the small group discussion, come back into the larger group. Look back at the Bible study portion of this chapter and share your list of do's and dont's for helping people in crises. Then, as a group, think back over this whole chapter and compose another list of Do's and Don't's for crisis helping. Record the group list on the following page.

Do	Don't

If time permits, discuss the following questions.

DISCUSSION QUESTIONS

1. What are the most important things to remember about a) the characteristics of people in a crisis, and b) how we can help people in a crisis?

2. *How to Be a People Helper* identifies two kinds of crises: developmental and accidental. Do you think either of these is worse than the other? Why? In what ways would your help in a developmental crisis differ from the help you would give in an accidental crisis?

3. At the graveside of Lazarus, Jesus dealt with a crisis. Can you think of other Biblical crisis-solving situations? What can we learn from these situations about our own crisis helping?

WHERE DO WE GO FROM HERE?

During this coming week, try to be alert to crisis situations around you. Are there neighbors, relatives, people at work, or fellow worshipers who are facing crises? If the opportunity arose, how would you help? Ask yourself the same question concerning the crises reported in newspapers.

In our next session we will be doing another role play which we want to record. *One member of each role-play group should bring a cassette recorder and tape.*

EXTRA ASSIGNMENT

An extra role-play session would be helpful, during which the helpee plays the role of someone in a crisis.

You might also want to read chapter 5 of the author's book *Effective Counseling* (Carol Stream, Illinois: Creation House, 1972). This chapter discusses counseling of mentally ill, physically ill, dying, grieving, physically disabled, and disadvantaged persons. See also chapters 3 and 4 of David K. Switzer's *The Minister as Crisis Counselor* (Nashville, Tennessee: Abingdon Press, 1974).

7
CAN YOU HELP OVER THE TELEPHONE?

When he invented the telephone, Alexander Graham Bell gave us a remarkable instrument—an invention which enables us to make verbal contact with people almost anywhere in the world, and all within a few seconds. It is true, of course, that the telephone can be annoying. Sometimes it rings too much or at inconvenient times, and it provides a means whereby our privacy can be interrupted at any hour of the day or night.

But the telephone also puts us into contact with people around us, and it enables those in need of help to find a helper quickly and easily. It would be impossible even to guess how many people are helped in times of need because of the nearness of the telephone. Effective counseling via the telephone requires some unique skills, however, and it is to these that we turn in the following pages.

GETTING STARTED BY LOOKING TO THE BIBLE

One need not be a Bible scholar to realize that we have no Biblical examples of telephone counseling! There are many instances, however, of people helping that took place from a distance. One of these is found in Matthew 11. Read verses 1-5 and then answer the following questions.

Who was in need of the help? _____

What was the problem? _____

Who was the people helper? _____

What did he do to help?_____

Perhaps the best examples of helping from a distance are found in Paul's letters to the various churches in the early Christian world. Note, in passing, that it is possible to help people by letter, although this is even more difficult than counseling either in person or by phone. Can you think of reasons for this statement?

Now turn to the book of 1 Corinthians in the New Testament and look at chapter 7. Notice that in verse 1 the Apostle Paul was writing to answer some questions that had been raised by the Corinthians in an earlier letter. The first question dealt with sex, and the writer's answer is given in verses 2-5.

According to one Bible scholar, this passage has been "grossly misunderstood." It has sometimes been cited as proof that Paul was a "warped and twisted man who hated women and despised marriage." William Barclay, the Scottish theologian, has commented on this in a perceptive way. In replying to the Corinthians' letter, Barclay writes,

> Paul's answer was extremely practical. In effect he said, "Remember where you are living; remember that you are living in Corinth, where you cannot even walk along the street without temptation rearing its head at you. Remember your own physical constitution and the healthy instincts which nature has given you. You will be far better to marry than to fall into sin." This sounds like a low view of marriage. It sounds as if Paul was advising marriage in order to avoid a worse fate. In point of fact he is sternly and honestly facing the facts. He is laying down a rule which is universally true. No man should attempt a way of life for which he is naturally unfitted; no man should set out on a pathway whereby he has deliberately surrounded himself with temptations. Paul knew very well that all men are not made in the same way. "Examine yourself," he says, "and choose that way of life in which you can best live the Christian life, and don't attempt an unnatural standard which is impossible and even wrong, for you being such as you are."

What has all of this got to do with helping, by letter or telephone, in the twentieth century? It illustrates some problems that are faced both in Bible study and in counseling:

1. It is difficult to understand a problem when we don't have all of the facts. The Corinthian Christians were surrounded by people who had the idea that "the body is unimportant; therefore it doesn't matter what we do with it." For some this was an excuse for engaging in all kinds of sexual excesses. For others there was an attempt to deny the instincts and pretend that natural desires of the body did not exist. Presumably Paul knew of this background when he wrote this letter, but often we as helpers do not have all of the needed facts. This makes telephone and written helping especially difficult. The helper is cut off from nonverbal clues that might be picked up in a face-to-face interview.

2. It is easy to be misunderstood by helpees when they cannot watch us face-to-face or have their questions answered immediately. One reason why 1 Corinthians 7 is misunderstood is that many people think this teaches the Biblical view of marriage in general. But here Paul was trying to deal with a specific problem in the light of unusual circumstances that the Corinthians faced (1 Cor. 7:26). Helpees (and helpers too) are likely to hear only what they want to hear, and this can create great misunderstanding.

In counseling from a distance, we must make a special effort to understand, to empathize, and to show warmth and genuineness by our words and by our tone of voice if we are talking by phone. We must also be alert to the possibility that helpees are more likely to misunderstand us when we are not present physically.

READING

Read chapter 6 of *How to Be a People Helper*.

Curt Wennerdahl, a psychiatric social worker in Grayslake, Illinois, has had considerable experience in the training of telephone counselors. The following paragraphs are adapted with permission from Mr. Wennerdahl's unpublished paper entitled "Ideas for Phone Workers."

Telephone callers have an uncanny skill in getting you to accept responsibility for their own problems, and soon you wind up becoming frustrated because you cannot produce a miracle solution. "I wish I could have done more," you think, and you may then begin to feel guilty and inadequate because you supposedly have not done your job. It is more helpful to constantly focus the responsibility back onto the caller by helping him to explore possible solutions for himself. It is rarely helpful for you to take over the responsibility for someone else's life.

Remember that it is usually very productive to help the caller explore his feelings about the situation he is presenting. When focusing on feelings, one need not be too concerned about whether or not the caller's stories are true. Sometimes, however, there is an exception to the above. When a caller is extremely distraught and upset, it is not particularly helpful to focus on feelings. It is better to take the opposite approach and focus on specific details of events in his life situation. This will often have a calming effect on the caller. Ask such questions as "Why don't you tell me what just happened?" or "Why don't we take one thing at a time and you tell me about it." To keep things moving, you might often add, "What happened next?" This approach can have definite structuring effect for a person who feels that his world is totally falling apart.

Do not hesitate to comment on suicidal clues. Some reference to suicide might well be implied in any of the following statements: "Sometimes I feel like running away from everything." "All I want to do is sleep." "Sometimes I think it would be better for everyone if I were not here." If you hear such a clue, you might say, "Have you ever been so upset that you thought of hurting yourself?" Do not ever be afraid to get the person to talk in detail about his or her suicidal thoughts. It is totally a myth to believe that if you talk about it, you will encourage a person to do it. This is absolutely not the case.

Remember that regardless of what a caller is talking about, he is also telling you something about himself. For example, even though a mother may be talking about her children, she is telling you something about herself. She may be saying, "Think of me as a mother who is feeling defeated." Further, she may be asking you to tell her that she is not so bad after all. When a person is talking to you about the details of his or her life, ask yourself, "What is he or she telling me right now about himself as a person?"

In some situations a person may attempt to put you on, perhaps by asking you questions about your own life in a provocative way, or in talking about sexual material. This often has a distancing effect (putting a distance between the caller and you). You may want to explore with the caller how he distances other people in his life. It also may be helpful to give him feedback as to how you are experiencing his attempt to put you on. Again, remember that he is telling you something about himself regardless of the way he is coming across to you. When you respond to what he is doing to you, this has the effect of keeping you unhooked from the content of his presentation. Remember also that you have the prerogative to set distinct limits for callers, both in terms of time and the type of material that you are willing to discuss with them.

Try not to get into the bind of expending great amounts of energy to get the caller to feel better. This often takes the form of actually trying to argue him out of his bad feelings by presenting all of the rosy things in life. A more helpful approach is to explore the bad feelings and perhaps talk about what they might be doing for the person in a positive way. For example, one might more appreciate the good times having experienced bad times. Also, one might be of more help to one's friends having experienced low feelings himself. In addition, sometimes bad feelings provide a rest from a demanding schedule. It is regretful that in life we sometimes develop symptoms in order to say "I need a rest" or "I need some space between other people and me." All of this has the quality of accepting the person together with his bad feelings. Otherwise you get into the bind of conveying to people that you will only accept them if they don't have bad feelings. There is something very powerful about not trying to argue people out of their feelings. One can assume that most callers have had numerous people in their environment trying to give them hundreds of solutions in order to feel better. You as a phone worker can be different; you can provide a different approach, which I suspect in most cases will be much more helpful than the dimestore variety solutions that people get from others.

Following are some suggestions for terminating a call.

1. "I think we've talked long enough. You might want to think about the alternatives we've talked about, and call back if you have further thoughts."

2. "I'm feeling rather drained and I would like to stop now."

3. "It seems to me that you have a lot to think about, and I don't feel it would be helpful to talk further at this time."

4. "I think you have at least these alternatives. Why don't you give each one of them some thought?"

When working with people on specific alternatives and choices in their lives, the following questions have proved quite helpful.

1. What is least likely to happen if you choose this alternative?

2. What is most likely to happen if you choose this alternative?

3. What will probably happen if you choose this alternative?

These three questions have proven quite helpful in getting the caller to look at the possible outcomes of a particular choice. Also, they have a way of bringing order to what might seem to be a very confusing situation.

PERSONAL EXERCISES

One of the essentials of people helping is that we learn to deal with very specific issues. Consider, for example, the following: "This has been a lousy day."

Such a statement is *vague*. It gives no indication why the day was lousy and it doesn't give the helper much information. The following statement is more *concrete* and *specific*: "I've had a headache all day today, the telephone has been ringing a lot more than usual, and there have been so many interruptions that I've hardly accomplished a thing."

People helpers must help others to speak concretely about themselves—their ideas, their feelings, their activities, and the events in their lives. This is important in all helping, but especially when we are talking on the telephone and unable to get clues about the helpee by watching him. Before helping others to be concrete and specific, however, we must learn how to speak concretely about ourselves.

1. Let us begin with feelings. In the spaces provided write a vague statement about your feelings (e.g., "I feel discouraged a lot"; "I feel guilty when I don't get things done"). Then rewrite the statement in more specific terms.

(a) vague statement about feelings _____

_____

specific statement _____

_____

(b) vague statement about feelings _____

specific statement _____

2. Now try the same exercise with your thinking (e.g., "I think this book is ridiculous" or "I think people are basically selfish").

(a) vague statement about thinking _____

specific statement _____

(b) vague statement about thinking _____

specific statement _____

3. Now repeat the exercise in terms of behavior or actions (e.g., "I mess things up sometimes" or "I can be pretty nasty").

(a) vague statement about behavior _____

specific statement _____

(b) vague statement about behavior _____

specific statement _____

4. As a final exercise, pretend that you are the helper and that one or more helpees make the *vague* statements that you have written above. In each case what would you say in order to get a more concrete statement from the helpee? (E.g., "Could you tell me more?"; "What is there about the book that makes it seem ridiculous?" or "You say you're nasty—in what ways?")

(1a) _____

_____

(1b) _____

_____

(2a) _____

_____

(2b) _____

_____

(3a) _____

_____

(3b) _____

_____

MEETING TOGETHER

This time we will do another role play in our small groups, but it will differ from the previous role plays in several ways.

First, we will do the role play at the beginning of our session together. *Following* the role play you will listen to the tape (not before).

Second, the helpee today should attempt to present a crisis-type situation. Perhaps something from the chart which you completed in the previous unit would be appropriate.

Third, in order to make the situation resemble a telephone interview, the helpee and helper should not look at each other during the interview. This is most conveniently done by sitting back-to-back or in some other way which permits the participants to hear but not to see each other.

Fourth, the session today should be recorded on a cassette tape. This might be difficult in view of the helper-helpee seating arrangement but it can be done.

Limit your role-play session to thirty minutes or less. A Role Play Rating Scale appears on page 113 of this book.

Now listen to the tape. You may want to take notes in the space below.

P _____

_____

U _____

_____

S _____

_____

I _____

_____

E _____

_____

A _____

_____

In the few minutes that remain, listen to your role-play tapes and decide what kinds of responses the helper was using.

DISCUSSION QUESTIONS

1. In the Bible study section of this unit, it was stated that helping people by letter or by telephone is more difficult than face-to-face counseling. Why is this so?

2. Can you think of reasons why vague statements are more difficult to deal with than specific, concrete statements?

3. *How to Be a People Helper* lists six "attitudes to avoid" or "games people helpers play." Are these always bad? How can we avoid these games?

WHERE DO WE GO FROM HERE?

Do you want to apply your telephone skills? You can start by being alert to the needs of friends when they call on the telephone. Without making a pest of yourself you might also call one or two people who are having problems and ask how things are going. In addition, look around your neighborhood and into the phonebook. Many communities have "telephone hotlines," "crisis telephone answering services," "contact teleministry," or other telephone counseling centers. Often these phones are staffed by volunteers. If you have an interest in being a volunteer, it is usually possible to get training for this and to get it free. Call the telephone counseling service in your community and ask how you can be a volunteer.

EXTRA ASSIGNMENT

Listen to the tape from the role play. Was the helpee vague in his or her statements, or was he concrete? How could the helper have responded differently, in a way that would have brought forth more concrete and specific responses?

8
WHERE DO YOU GO WHEN YOU NEED HELP?

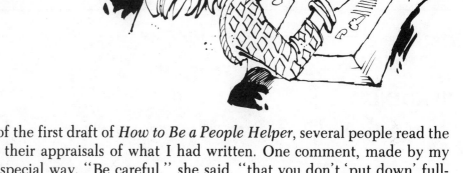

Shortly after completion of the first draft of *How to Be a People Helper*, several people read the manuscript and gave me their appraisals of what I had written. One comment, made by my wife, stuck with me in a special way. "Be careful," she said, "that you don't 'put down' full-time counselors."

Certainly counselors vary in their competence, and in many cases lay helpers can do at least as effective a job as some professionals. But this is not to distract from the experience and know-how of those persons whose training and vocation have led them into the field of professional counseling. These people can be of great help to the nonprofessional, and often we will want to refer one of our helpees to an expert. When and how to make such referrals, and where we can get professional guidance in our work, are the concerns of this unit.

GETTING STARTED BY LOOKING TO THE BIBLE

The best Biblical example of referral is found in Exodus 18. Read the entire chapter.

Who are the two key people in this chapter? _____ _____

What was the reason for these two people meeting? _____

_____

What two things did Jethro notice about his son-in-law?

(a) verses 8-12 _____

_____

(b) verses 13, 14 _____

_____

What concerned Jethro about Moses' people helping activities (verses 14, 17, 18)?

_____

What was Jethro's advice (verses 19-22)? _____

_____

What were to be the characteristics of the lay people helpers (verse 21)?

_____

_____

What was to be referred to another person (verse 22, 26)? _____

_____

What does this say to you about referrals? _____

_____

_____

READING

Please read chapter 7 in *How to Be a People Helper*.

PERSONAL EXERCISES

We have two tasks before us in this unit. The first deals with suicide, and the second introduces something called *immediacy*, which is another kind of helping skill.*

1.   It is possible to learn much about suicide by reading suicide notes. The following are suicide notes originally published in a book by E. S. Shneidman and N. L. Farberow (*Clues to-Suicide*. New York: McGraw-Hill, 1957). For each pair of notes, one is authentic (written by a person who subsequently committed suicide), and the other is not real. Read the first five pairs of notes and decide which of the notes you think is accurate. Record your answers on page 114 in the back of the book.

1A   To the Police. No note—one was written before this. Los Angeles Police already have a record of one attempt. Notify—Anne M. Jones, 100 Main St., Los Angeles, Tel. BA 0-0000. I live at 100 Spring St. Los Angeles. I work at Ford, 100 Broadway. That is all.
I can't find my place in life.

J. William Smith

1B   Dear Mom, In the last week a number of occurrances have forced me into a position where I feel my life is not worth continuing.
Friday I lost the job I have held for the past seven years. When I told my wife she packed her bags and left me. For six years she has been living with me, not for me but for my money.
Mom please take care of Mary for me. I'm leaving and I don't want Betty to have her. I have nothing left to live for so I'm just checking out.

I love you Mom, Bill

---

* The first of these exercises is adapted from Gary R. Collins, Peter S. Fernald, and L. Dodge Fernald, Jr., *Instructor's Manual to Accompany Introduction to Psychology, 2nd Edition* (Boston: Houghton-Mifflin, 1969). The second exercise is adapted from Gerard Egan, *Exercises in Helping Skills* (Monterey, California: Brooks/Cole, 1975).

2A   I hope this is what you wanted.

2B   Dear, please forgive me for leaving you with all the responsibilities that this is certain to bring on you. If there is anything of me that can be used in any medical or scientific way please don't refuse to let them as my last request. I am very proud of our son, and his high potential in his chosen field for which he has real talent. Bye for the last time, and never forget that you were the best thing that ever happened to me. Have my brother help you, I know he will want to very much.

3A   I am tired of living so I decided to end it all, hope this will not distress anybody.

3B   Dearest Mary. This is to say goodbye. I have not told you because I did not want you to worry, but I have been feeling bad for 2 years, with my heart. I knew that if I went to a doctor I would lose my job. I think this is best for all concerned. I am in the car in the garage. Call the police but please don't come out there. I love you very much darling. Goodbye,

Bill

4A   Dear Mary. You have been the best wife a man could want and I still love you after fifteen years.
      Don't think to badly of me for taking this way out but I can't take much more pain and sickness also I may get too much pain or so weak that I can't go this easy way. With all my love forever—

Bill

4B   Goodbye dear wife. I cannot stand the suffering any longer. I am doing this by my own free will. You will be well taken care of.

Love and goodbye

5A   My Darling: I'm sorry to leave you this way, but it looks like the only way out for me. Things have become so uncertain and unbearable, that I believe it will be better this way. Have the kids remember me, and don't be grievous because I took this way out. Never forget that I love you with all my heart and soul.

Bill

5B   Dear Mother. I just cannot take it any more this is no way out but this has me down. I Joseph William Smith give everything to Henry Jones my car and what ever I have.

Joseph Smith

In their book, Shneidman and Farberow describe a study in which they matched real suicide notes with those which were not real. They concluded that in general

> Thirty-three writers of authentic suicide notes were matched man-for-man, according to age, occupation, race, marital status and other variables, with thirty-three nonsuicidal, simulated-suicide-note writers, and the following differences in their notes were observed. Generally speaking, the authentic notes were longer and contained a slightly larger percentage of statements pertaining to negative emotions, such as anger and guilt. No differences were noted in the percentage of statements about positive emotions, such as love, but the authentic notes contained a much greater percentage of emotionally neutral statements. Inspection of the later statements indicated that many contained instructions and admonitions and sometimes listed things to do.

With this background in mind, read the next five pairs of notes, recording your answers on page 114.

6A   Dear Mary. I'm sorry for all the trouble I've caused you. I guess I can't say any more. I love you forever and give Tom my love. I guess I've disgraced myself and John I hope it doesn't reflect on you.

6B   Darling: It's been great but I just can't go on for reasons you may know but I can't explain. There's enough insurance for all of you. Be happy and all my love always to you and our three.

Remember me as your adoring

Bill

7A   Dear Wife; I am sorry to cause you this embarrassment but I can't seem to stand life this way. This is the easy way for me. You will get over it in time too.

7B   Dearest Mary—I just can't go on without Tom, John and you. I hope some day you can forgive me. I know you will find someone better for you and the boys. God bless you all.

Love, Bill

8A   I'm tired of being sick and in pain and can see no use in prolonging it as they say there is no hope of recovery.

8B   I specifically request that my body be disposed of by cremation. To my good friends, Joe Smith and Mary Jones I give my deep and undying affection. My dear parents, Henry W. and Betty C. Brown have done their best for me and it is my failure, rather than anything they have failed to offer that has brought this about. My sister, Helen White of 100 Main Street, New York, is closest and dearest to me and, with her consent, I ask that she take and raise my son. My phonograph records, now in storage with my parents, I give to my former wife, Wilma Brown, 200 Broadway, Los Angeles, Calif.

Explanations would be useless, suffice to say I have tried and failed. Given unto my hand this ninth day of June in the year of 1943, A.D., in the city of Los Angeles, California.

Jack Brown

9A   Some where in this pile is your answers. I couldn't find it. Mom, you should have known what was about to happen after I told you my troubles now I will get my rest.

Dad, I am in this jam because I trusted people (namely you) and some people trusted me, because I am, in my present state a menace to me and my customers I think this is the best way out, and out of my insurance if you ever take a drink I hope you drown yourself with it.

9B   Dear Mary. Things are piling up too high for me. I love you but I know our basic difficulties are not soluable. Please don't think too harshly of me if I take this way out. You have insurance and your health to help get started again. Tell the kids I had an accident so they wont be ashamed of their daddy.

Love, Bill

10A   To the police. please tell family that I love them why say more.

10B   Good by Kid. You couldn't help it. Tell that brother of yours, When he gets where I'm going. I hope I'm a foreman down there, I might be able to do something for him.

Bill

The authentic suicide notes are as follows: 1A, 2A, 3B, 4A, 5B, 6A, 7B, 8B, 9A, 10B.

How many of the notes did you identify correctly? Did your accuracy improve on the last five pairs (after you read about the Shneidman-Farberow study)? What have these notes taught you about helping suicidal people?

_____

_____

_____

_____

2.   According to Gerard Egan, *immediacy* refers to the helper's ability to discuss with the helpee exactly what is going on between them as they talk. "You're not being honest with me,"

"I feel very uncomfortable with you right now," "I'm not convinced that your counseling is helping me," "You don't seem to have much interest in what I'm saying"—these are examples of immediacy responses.

Immediacy discussions can make communication easier, and they enable the helpee to understand himself or herself better. However, it is difficult to talk on such an intimate level, feelings can be hurt, and sometimes the helper-helpee relationship can be hurt.

The following exercise adapted from Egan, plus the group meeting activities which follow, should give you the feel of immediacy.

Read the following examples:

(a) College student speaking to girlfriend:
"We don't seem to be getting anywhere in our relationship. When I've called you recently you've always seemed to be too busy to talk, and sometimes I find our dates to be rather boring. I don't know about you, but this is making me feel pretty frustrated. Maybe you see our relationship differently."

(b) Helper talking to helpee:
"You didn't like what I just said, did you? We seem to get along okay until I mention something about religion, and then I think you clam up and get angry with me. Does this make sense to you?"

(c) Wife to husband:
"Have you noticed that we're arguing more than we used to? We don't discuss issues like we used to. Instead, it seems that whenever we disagree, we keep things hidden, let our anger burn, and then blow up like we did this morning."

Think of some people in your life with whom you would like to talk openly about the relationship between you. In the space provided, indicate what you might say to open an immediacy discussion between you. In each case, share something about your feelings on the matter, say what you think about the current status of the relationship, try to be specific, and invite that other person to respond.

1. Person being addressed: _____

    Immediacy response _____

    _____

    _____

    _____

2. Person being addressed: _____

    Immediacy response _____

    _____

    _____

    _____

Now write out an immediacy response for each member of your role-play group.

3. Person being addressed: _____

    Immediacy response _____

    _____

4. Person being addressed: _____

   Immediacy response _____

   _____

   _____

   _____

5. Person being addressed: _____

   Immediacy response _____

   _____

MEETING TOGETHER

Once again we will begin with a role play and listen to the tape later. A Role Play Rating Scale appears on page 115, near the end of this book.

If possible, try to include an immediacy response or two within the role-play situation. If the situation can lend itself to this, the helper might also try to suggest the idea of referral.

Following the role play, listen to the tape. You may want to jot down a few notes below.

_____

_____

_____

_____

_____

_____

_____

_____

_____

_____

_____

DISCUSSION QUESTIONS

1. What can you as a helper do if your helpee is suicidal but refuses to be referred to a professional? What if there is no professional counselor to whom you can make a referral?

2. What and how might you refer people in your community?

3. What are the values of immediacy responses? What are the dangers?

WHERE DO WE GO FROM HERE?

Give some thought to why people, including Christians, attempt suicide.

It might help in the future if you start keeping a list of places and people in your community to whom you could refer your helpers.

Try using immediacy responses outside your role-play and people helping sessions. Could this type of communication be beneficial to a marriage, a discussion between friends, or an interaction between church members and church leaders?

EXTRA ASSIGNMENT

An excellent volume on suicide, written from a Christian perspective, is that of D. Lumm, *Responding to Suicidal Crises* (Grand Rapids: Eerdmans, 1974). You may wish to read all or part of this book.

9

CAN PROBLEMS BE STOPPED BEFORE THEY START?

Many of the authors who write about preventing problems make reference to an old example of the cliff and the rescue station. Counseling, it is suggested, exists to help people who are in trouble. Like the rescue station at the bottom of a cliff, counseling picks up those who have fallen and are in need of help getting back on their feet. Might it be better, these writers ask, if we dispatched part of the rescue squad to the top of the cliff to build fences so people wouldn't fall in the first place? This fence-building is what we mean by prevention: stopping problems before they start or catching a person who is slipping before he or she gets hurt.

GETTING STARTED BY LOOKING TO THE BIBLE

There are many places in the Bible where people are warned about dangers and are given help for anticipating problems. Look, for example, at each of the following to see if you can identify some problem-stopping technique. The first example has been done for you. You may have other examples to add at the end of this list.

Scripture	*Prevention Technique*
Genesis 2:17	*warning of what not to do and of the consequences of disobedience.*
1 Kings 19:1-8	
Psalm 55:22	
Psalm 119:9-11	
Proverbs 3:5, 6	
Proverbs 16:3, 9	
Proverbs 21:13; 22:9	
Romans 12:1, 2	

72

2 Timothy 2:15 _____

James 1:19 _____

James 5:16 _____

1 John 1:9 _____

_____ _____

_____ _____

_____ _____

Turn now to Matthew chapter 10 and read the entire chapter. This is background information for the reading which follows.

READING

Read chapter 8 of *How to Be a People Helper*.

The following excerpt is taken from the author's book *Effective Counseling* (Carol Stream, Illinois: Creation House, 1972), pp. 172-80. In writing this I drew heavily on Howard J. Clinebell's book *Mental Health through Christian Community* (Nashville: Abingdon, 1965).

While establishing mental health in the community is not the church's primary role, if we believe that the Christian message has relevance to the needs of contemporary men, then we are responsible for bringing Christianity's resources to bear on the problems of those in our congregations and communities. There are at least nine practical ways in which church leaders can do this; all are consistent with biblical revelation and psychologically sound:

Introduce men to Jesus Christ. The Bible does not promise that Christianity is a ticket to permanent mental health. The follower of Jesus Christ must bear a cross (Mt. 16:24; Mk. 8:34; 10:21; Lk. 9:23) and commit himself to a costly form of discipleship. Becoming a Christian often creates problems we could otherwise avoid. Why, then, should we encourage men and women to invite Christ into their lives? One reason is that by following Christ we have a challenging purpose in life (to follow Him) and a reason for living (Mt. 16:24-25; 2 Cor. 5:15, 17; Gal. 2:20; Phil. 1:21). In addition, belief in Christ gives us "enduring faith" and a basis for the values that many psychologists consider to be so important. In times of crises, Jesus Christ gives support and encouragement to those who depend on Him (Mt. 11:28-30). Indeed, the whole Christian life is one of fullness (Mk. 1:15; Jn. 10:10) and has been the experience of believers for centuries. Then, when we approach the end of life, we can face death knowing that there is eternal existence in a place

prepared for those who have believed that Jesus Christ is the Son of God (Jn. 14:1-3; 3:16).

Worship. In the Old Testament, the worship of God was a central act in the life of the people. During His life on earth, Jesus reaffirmed the importance of worship both with His words (Matt. 4:10*b*; John 4:23) and His example (Luke 4:16). The early church worshiped together (Acts 2:47); Paul encouraged believers to pray and give thanks (1 Tim. 2:1); Peter and the writer of Hebrews instructed us to give praise (1 Pet. 2:9; Heb. 13:15); and the book of the Revelation indicates that worship will be a part of the future (4:10-11; 5:8-14; 7:9-12).

Worship is more than a divine commandment, however; it is an experience which encourages good mental health. For many, worship gives a feeling of oneness with others. As people sing in unison, pray together, and draw near to God, they also draw closer to each other and feel less isolated. Worship that is reverent gives an awareness of God's presence, a renewed sense of trust, a feeling of superhuman strength, and an opportunity to sit quietly and reflect.

Too often worship in the local church is not a meaningful experience, but is instead a dull, mechanical routine. In many churches—especially evangelical Protestant churches—there is considerable chatter (which we call "fellowship") before, after, and sometimes during the services. The minister shows little sense of reverence and the people are deprived of an experience which could be spiritually uplifting and psychologically invigorating. Perhaps this is partly what Dr. Karl Menninger, the famous psychiatrist, had in mind recently when he said, "If only we could get clergymen to appreciate what a marvelous opportunity for group therapy they let slip through their fingers every Sunday morning!"

Private devotions. Here is another activity which was a vital part of the life of Jesus (Mark 1:35; 6:46-47; Luke 6:12) and is a must for every one of His followers (Ps. 46; 1 Thess. 5:17; 1 Tim. 2:8; John 5:39). Prayer gives us strength (1 Chron. 16:11; Luke 18:1), wisdom (Matt. 7:7; James 1:5), the ability to withstand temptations (Matt. 26:41), joy (John 16:24), the opportunity to express our feelings (James 5:13), and the material things that we need and that God wants us to have (1 John 5:14-15; James 4:2-3; Matt. 21:22). Quiet meditation and study of the Scriptures give us knowledge, confidence, and hope (2 Tim. 2:15; John 5:39; Rom. 15:4).

In this age of hyperactivity and excessive busyness, men need to be still and get to know God (Ps. 46:10). Such a quiet time is another example of behavior which is of crucial importance, both spiritually and psychologically.

Preaching. Harry Emerson Fosdick once described preaching as "personal counseling on a group scale." While this is a somewhat limited definition, it is true that the sermon can be a great opportunity for stimulating mental health. As he seeks to proclaim the Word of God, the preacher must show how the truths of the Bible apply to men's needs and everyday problems of living. The pulpit is no place for political discussions, airing of pet peeves, clichés, pompous irrelevant jargon, or messages which fail to relate to the needs of men. The sermon which Peter preached on the day of Pentecost (Acts 2) is a good example of speaking to men's needs, showing the relevance of Scripture, and giving opportunity for men to make a practical response to the Word of God.

Teaching. The hour between 10 and 11 on Sunday morning has been called the "most wasted hour of the week." Thousands of youngsters are bored with Sunday school programs and become church dropouts as soon as they can get out from under parental pressure to attend. But the Christian education program is vital to the work of the church and can make a valuable contribution to mental health. But, to be effective, it must be reevaluated in many local congregations.

Numerous church members, denominational leaders, and specialists in the field of Christian education have been engaged in this evaluation,

and as a result the church's teaching ministry has improved greatly. To make a contribution to the mental health of church members, Christian educators can clearly teach the facts of one's faith, since this gives grounding in a belief system and a sense of security in knowing where one stands; can provide stimulation and challenge, since this is necessary for normal development; can guide in the development of values and a philosophy of life; can teach appreciation for the importance of consistent worship, meditation, prayer, and personal Bible study; can discuss contemporary personal problems in the light of Scripture; can consider such practical matters as one's vocation, family communication, relationships with the opposite sex, and marriage; can provide opportunity for close interaction with other people; can alert us to potential problems; and can provide opportunity for counseling.

Stimulating healthy family life. Most abnormal behavior can be traced back to an unhealthy family situation. Many research studies have shown that early experience in the home is of crucial importance, and even wise King Solomon recognized the importance of early training and discipline (Prov. 22:6; 13:24).

A healthy family is one which is characterized by love, mutual respect, communication, discipline, and religious training. In addition it is important that there be stimulation with such things as toys, books, activity, physical contacts, and verbal interaction with others. To foster this kind of environment, churches might consider the use of sermons that deal with the family, discussions or Bible-study groups which consider family relationships, premarital guidance, discussions with young married couples or young parents, and family counseling. It is also important that church activities not encourage family fragmentation. While graded Christian education classes are desirable, we must not split the church into so many specialized groups that there will be no opportunity for families to be together. To avoid this problem, some churches hold all of their weekly meetings on one night. Families participate together in a church dinner, and then the members disperse to their various age-group activities.

Group interaction. There are many things that a person can do alone, but being a Christian is not one of them. Jesus had a little band of twelve disciples whom He trained (Matt. 10) and sent forth as witnesses. The early church was a closely knit group that met together for study, fellowship, the "breaking of bread," and prayer (Acts 2:42). The first missionary journeys were made by teams of men. Over the centuries it has become apparent that the training of small groups has been a part of every major surge of spiritual vitality in the church.

Within the past few years churches have shown a renewed interest in small groups. Christians have discovered that there is real spiritual growth when two or more people get together to pray, study, discuss, and share their personal needs or concerns. Group experience gives a feeling of "we-ness." It shows that somebody cares, and it gives us an opportunity to be concerned about others. In an age of great mobility, the church group gives people a "family" and a feeling of rootedness wherever they go. It provides support in times of crises, friends in times of loneliness, and advice in times of indecision. In the small group we can learn how to relate to people and observe how others respond to us. Best of all, the Christian group draws us closer to God, for "where two or three are gathered together in my name," Jesus stated, "there am I in the midst of them" (Matt. 18:20).

Church groups are usually formed to fulfill one or more of the following tasks: study, prayer, work and service, mutual sharing of problems, and fellowship. While some of these tasks may be more therapeutic than others, all can contribute to better mental and spiritual health. It should be remembered, however, that people today are too busy to get involved in still another club or activity unless they can see that the group will have genuine relevance. To insure this, the churchman should have a good understanding of how groups work as well as some skill in group leadership.

Service. The gospel accounts indicate that Jesus spent much time in private communion with God, and that He devoted many hours to teaching His little group of disciples. But Jesus also was highly involved in service to others. He healed the sick, ministered to the needy, and preached from the Scriptures. Clearly He expects His followers to do likewise (Matt. 20:7-8; 28:19-20; Titus 3:8). A faith that does not lead men to do good works is a faith that is dead (James 2:17-18).

The therapeutic value of service to others was discovered early by members of Alcoholics Anonymous, who found that by helping others they helped themselves. God has given men different gifts (Rom. 12; 1 Cor. 12), and undoubtedly we have different responsibilities. We are called to difficult occupations and various places of work, but no Christian is completely excused from service. The church, therefore, must encourage and mobilize the laborers. Guided by the Holy Spirit, our service will reach others and, in turn, help us both spiritually and psychologically.

Support in crises. In the United States and Canada it is considered bad manners to look closely at people in public. We are taught to respect the privacy of others and to avoid staring—even when we want very much to do so. If other people are suffering or in need of help, we still pass by on the other side and pretend not to see. The psychotic is often dismissed as an "oddball" and rejected by his own family, while patients who are dying find that their friends and even hospital personnel avoid the sickroom. Apparently many of us are embarrassed and uncomfortable when in the presence of suffering and need.

But people who are facing crises need the help of others. The physically and mentally ill, the discouraged, bereaved, rejected, aged, and the families of such people all need support and encouragement. As followers of Christ, who is always present when we are in need (Matt. 11:20, 28-30), Christians are failing in their duty if they neglect to minister to those facing the crises of life.

PERSONAL EXERCISES

By now it should be apparent that there are many ways by which we can prevent problems. One technique that we have not mentioned, a technique that is also helpful in counseling, is the use of confrontation.

We might think of confrontation as the uncovering of sins, inconsistencies, evasive behavior, discrepancies, self-defeating ideas or behavior, and anything else which helpees use to avoid facing their problems and changing their actions. In his widely popular book *Competent to Counsel*, Adams puts confrontation at the center of his approach, though Jesus used a variety of other approaches. Most professionals would agree that "confrontation is a much-abused type of interaction," which is often destructive and sometimes overused, especially by inept and unskilled counselors.

In his book *The Skilled Helper* (Monterey, California: Brooks/Cole, 1975), Gerard Egan suggests that we should confront:

- in a spirit of empathy—making every effort to understand the helpee;
- tentatively—it may be that our perception of the other person's situation is wrong;
- with care—and caring;
- in an attitude of involvement—so that the helper is "with" the helpee;
- with a desire to help and motivate—not with the intention of punishing, getting even, or "putting down" the helpee;
- gradually—rather than hitting the helpee with a whole group of things which need changing;
- concretely—so that you mention specific things rather than something general and vague like "You don't interact effectively with others."

In the exercise which follows (adapted from Egan), we work on the assumption that the best way to learn confrontation is to begin with ourselves.

Think of two areas in your life for which some kind of challenge or confrontation might be beneficial. Then write out a statement in which you a) confront yourself irresponsibly (breaking all of Egan's suggestions listed above) and b) confront yourself responsibly (using Egan's guidelines).

EXAMPLE

(a) Irresponsible: Why don't you get up off your big rear and start doing something instead of sitting around moping all day. You never face any of your problems but expect other people to wait on you and give you all kinds of sympathy. No wonder you feel miserable. You cause most of your own problems and make everybody around you miserable too.

(b) Responsible: Let me check something out with you. You seem to be unhappy all the time and complain because other people don't help you or show sympathy. Might it be that you have slipped into a habit of doing nothing about your problems except to feel sorry for yourself? What would happen if we started working on some specific things which you could do to deal with your problems?

Self-Confrontation 1

(a) Irresponsible: _____

_____

_____

_____

(b) Responsible: _____

_____

_____

Self-Confrontation 2

    (a) Irresponsible: _____

_____

_____

_____

    (b) Responsible: _____

_____

_____

_____

MEETING TOGETHER

The tape includes a brief discussion of premarital and marriage counseling (thirteen minutes). You can take notes below.

_____

_____

_____

_____

_____

Now do another role play. A Role Play Rating Scale is found on page 116. Consistent with the theme of our discussion in this unit, you may want to try some preventive helping, perhaps premarital counseling.

If time permits, at the end of the session share the confrontation statements that you wrote above with other members of the role-play group. What is good about the responsible statements? How could they be improved?

DISCUSSION QUESTIONS

    1. Do you think it is ever wise to confront a helpee in a manner that we have labeled "irresponsible" above?

    2. What can you do specifically and at present to help others prevent problems?

    3. Are there things that you can do to prevent problems in your own life?

WHERE DO WE GO FROM HERE?

Think back to that example of the cliff and the rescue station. Most of our emphasis in this growthbook has been on the remedial helping of a rescue-station variety. It is important that we enlarge our perspective and give serious thought to the specific ways in which we can be involved in preventive helping.

EXTRA ASSIGNMENT

The author's book *Effective Counseling* (Carol Stream, Illinois: Creation House, 1972) has a chapter on "Premarital, Marital and Family Counseling" and another on "Mental Health and Prevention of Abnormality." For an excellent discussion on confrontation read Gerard Egan, *The Skilled Helper* (Monterey, California: Brooks/Cole, 1975), page 156 and following.

10
HOW
DO YOU
FIT IN
WITH OTHERS?

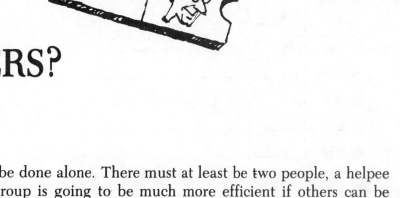

People helping, of course, cannot be done alone. There must at least be two people, a helpee and helper, and even this little group is going to be much more efficient if others can be involved in the helping process. This is where the church plays a vital role. It is a body of believers who possess a variety of special gifts and who need each other if individual members of the group are to be helped in the best possible way.

GETTING STARTED BY LOOKING TO THE BIBLE

In his best-selling book, *Body Life* (Ventura, California: Regal Books, 1972), Ray C. Stedman has pointed out that the Book of Ephesians, especially chapter 4, deals almost exclusively with the church. "The first aim of the church," writes Stedman, "is to live to the praise and glory of God . . . to declare in word and demonstrate in attitude and deed the character of Jesus Christ, who lives within his people . . . to declare the reality of life-changing encounter with a living Christ . . . to demonstrate that change by an unselfish, love-filled life . . . ." The church is primarily a body, a unified group of believers all of whom are under the authority of Christ.

"Under his direction the whole body is fitted together perfectly, and each part in its own special way helps the other parts, so that the whole body is healthy and growing and full of love" (Ephesians 4:16, *The Living Bible*)

This is a beautiful description of a healing-helping community. Under Christ's direction, the members of the body are to cooperate and help one another so that everyone experiences health, maturing, and love. This sounds ideal, but it need not be unrealistic or unattainable. It is a divine pattern to maximize helping.

Turn now to Ephesians chapter 4. Please read the entire chapter and then note below how the body of Christ (the church) can contribute to the people helping process. We begin by looking at Ephesians 4:1, where we read that Christians should walk (i.e., live a life) that reflects our being called as a follower of Jesus Christ. If you have difficulty filling in the spaces below, turn to page 117 of this book.

1. Characteristics of People Helpers in the Body (from Ephesians)

    (1:4) _____, _____

    (4:2) _____, _____, _____, _____

    (4:3) _____

    (4:26) _____

    (4:32) _____, _____, _____

2. Activities of People Helpers in the Body (from Ephesians)

    (4:12) _____

    (4:15) _____

    (4:22) _____

    (4:23) _____

    (4:24) _____

    (4:25) _____

    (4:26) _____

    (4:28) _____ , _____

    (4:29) _____ , _____

    (4:30) _____

    (4:31) _____, _____, _____, _____

    (4:32) _____, _____, _____

3. Goals of People Helpers in the Body (from Ephesians)

    (4:13) _____, _____, _____

    (4:14) _____

    (4:28) _____

    What does this have to do with your activities as a people helper? Be specific.

    _____

    _____

    _____

READING

The following is taken from Ray C. Stedman's book *Body Life*, to which we made reference above. As you read this ask yourself what it has to do with a) discipleship and b) people helping.

Bearing one another's burdens at the very least means to uphold one another in prayer. It also means to be willing to spend time with another person in thoroughly understanding his problem, and committing oneself to certain effort to relieve pressure or discouragement, or in finding some way to help financially or by wise counsel. Christians must not transfer such responsibility to governmental authorities, either national or local. Help available from such sources should be welcomed and used, but nothing can take the place of an arm around the shoulder, a repeated time of prayer together, or a steadying word of counsel from a brother or sister in the family of God.

Another direct exhortation from the Word is that of James 5:16: *Confess your sins one to another, and pray for one another, that you may be healed.* Confessing faults certainly means to admit weaknesses and to acknowledge failures in living as Christians. It is often difficult to get Christians to do this, despite the clear directive of the Word. It goes against the grain to give an image of oneself that is anything less than perfect, and many Christians imagine that they will be rejected by others if they admit to any faults. But nothing could be more destructive to Christian *koinonia* than the common practice today of pretending not to have any problems. It is often true that Christian homes may be filled with bickering, squabbling, angry tantrums, even bodily attacks of one member of the family against another, and yet not one word of this is breathed to anyone else, and the impression is carefully cultivated before other Christians that this is an ideal Christian family with no problems of any serious consequence to be worked out.

To make matters even worse, this kind of conspiracy of silence is regarded as the Christian thing to do, and the hypocrisy it presents to others (not to mention how it appears to individual members of the family) is considered to be part of the family's "witness" to the world. How helpful, how wonderfully helpful, it would be if one of the members of this family (preferably the father) would honestly admit in a gathering of fellow Christians that his family was going through difficulties in working out relationships with one another, and needed very much their prayers and counsel through this time of struggle. The family member would immediately discover at least two things: (1) that every other Christian in the meeting identified with his problem and held him in higher esteem than ever because of his honesty and forthrightness; and (2) a wealth of helpful counsel would be opened to him from those who had gone through similar struggles and had learned very valuable lessons thereby. Further, the prayers of other Christians willing to help him bear his burden would release great spiritual power into the situation, so that members of the family would be able to see much more clearly the issues to be resolved and be empowered to bear with patience and love the weaknesses of each other. The very next verse in the book of James, following the injunction to confess faults, is: "The prayer of a righteous man has great power in its effects."

It is most significant that whenever spiritual awakenings have occurred throughout the Christian centuries they have always been accompanied by a restoration of *koinonia*, of the confession of faults, and the bearing of one another's burdens. During the Wesleyan awakening in eighteenth century England, the great evangelist George Whitefield wrote to his converts:

"My brethren . . . let us plainly and freely tell one another what God has done for our souls. To this end you would do well, as others have done, to form yourselves into little companies of four or five each, and meet once a week to tell each other what is in your hearts, that you may then also pray for and comfort each other as need shall require. None but those who have experienced it can tell the unspeakable advantages of such a union and communion of souls . . . . None, I think, that truly loves his own soul and his brethren as himself will be shy of opening his heart, in order to have their advice, reproof, admonition, and prayers, as occasions require. A sincere person will esteem it one of the greatest blessings."

When this kind of sharing and burden-bearing is occurring in a church it will go far in relieving the load of counseling that elders or pastors must do. Many emotional and even mental problems would be solved at their beginnings through the genuine love and concern of other Christians and would never grow into the complicated tangles that now require long hours of skilled counseling to unravel. Modern techniques of group therapy are built on this same basic principle of a common sharing that the early church so richly enjoyed.

Obviously there are certain intimate or scandalous matters that should not be voiced in an open meeting. Some types of sharing should be done privately between only two or three individuals who are trustworthy and mature in their insights. But no Christian should bear a heavy burden alone. Those with the gift of encouragement should make themselves available to others for this ministry, and any who appear to be withdrawn or downcast should be gently encouraged to unload. The gift of a listening ear and an understanding heart is sometimes the greatest gift one Christian can give another. Essential to this matter of building up or edifying the body of Christ is the apostle's admonition in Ephesians 4:15: "speaking the truth in love." In the Greek it is simply "truthing in love." It has in its meaning not only speaking the truth but demonstrating it in every area of life.

Once again the common practice of Christians toward each other fails greatly at this point. We all tend to shy away from an unpleasant confrontation. If someone has an unpleasant or irritating habit or manner we are willing enough to talk about it to others but seldom say anything to the person directly. If we do, it is usually only when we have been angered or irritated to the point of sharp and caustic protest. Our reason for silence is most often that "we don't wish to hurt him." That, of course, is self-deception. It is ourselves that we don't wish to hurt by having to tell someone a painful truth. In actual fact we do the other person incalculable harm by our unloving silence, for we condemn him or her to go on offending others and suffering rejection without realizing what it is that is creating the problem. No one loves him enough to take him aside and lovingly and understandingly point out the offending practice. The worst thing of all is to baptize the silence and think of it as a mark of Christian love.

Yet every Christian has had occasion to be grateful beyond words for the loving admonition of some friend or brother who has helped him to see a blind spot and showed him how to lay hold of the grace of God to overcome an annoying and disagreeable habit. *Faithful are the wounds of a friend* (Prov. 27:6). We must again take most seriously the words of Galatians 6:1: *Brethren, if a man is overtaken in any fault, you who are spiritual should restore him in a spirit of gentleness, looking to yourself, lest you too be tempted.*

This is the ministry of washing one another's feet, which Jesus said was most necessary among his disciples: *If I, then, your Lord and Teacher, have washed your feet, you also ought to wash one another's feet. For I have given you an example, that you also should do as I have done to you* (John 13:14-15). That he meant this to be taken symbolically and not literally is seen in his words, *What I am doing you do not know now, but afterward you will understand* (John 13:7). One can never do this work of washing another's feet without taking the place of a servant, as our Lord did. But, as Dr. H. A. Ironside used to say,

it helps greatly to be careful of the temperature of the water we use! Some come to others with icy cold water and say, "Here, stick your feet in here." Their cold, forbidding attitude arouses only resentment. Others are so angry and upset themselves when they come that it is like offering to wash another's feet in boiling water. The only way is to come with warm water which makes the unpleasant task of footwashing as pleasurable as possible. The one thing we must not do is to turn away and leave the offending person unrestored and unhelped.

A healthy body is necessary to do effective work. To attempt evangelism while the body of Christ is sick and ailing is worse than useless. It is not difficult to keep a body of Christians healthy and vital if the individuals involved (especially leaders) are concerned to bear one another's burdens, confess their faults one to another, and to instruct and admonish one another in love by means of the Word of God. It is by these means that the church is becoming what its Lord desires: *a church in splendor, without spot or wrinkle or any such thing* (Eph. 5:27).

The work of the ministry, as we have seen, is directed toward a suffering and desperate world. It requires every member of the body of Christ to accomplish it effectively, as God intended it to be done. It also requires that the members of the body shall be spiritually healthy, vibrant with the life of Christ who indwells them through his Spirit.

No athlete spends all his time running races or playing the game for which he is trained; he must also spend many hours keeping himself in shape and developing his skills to a high degree. So it is also with the body of Christ. The work of the ministry will never be properly done by a weak and unhealthy church, torn with internal pains and wracked by spiritual diseases. Thus it is no surprise that the pattern of the Holy Spirit for the operation of Christ's body should indicate that apostles, prophets, evangelists, and pastor-teachers exist not only to equip the saints to the work of the ministry, but also to aid and support them in a mutual ministry to each other which results in *building up the body of Christ.*

Great damage has been done by unhealthy saints attempting to reach out to the world in evangelism or social help in spasms of dedicated zeal, but without true spiritual health. Burdened with unsolved problems in their own lives, and unconsciously displaying unresolved hypocrisies of prejudice and outlook, their spasmodic activities in evangelism or help seem to be but hollow mockeries of Christianity in the eyes of those they hope to reach. Their own Christian meetings have turned into dull, stodgy rituals where many Christians gather to go through completely predictable performances, all conducted in an atmosphere of "reverence" which permits no interchange with one another, no exchange of thought, no discussion of truth, and no opportunity to display Christian love in any but the most superficial of ways.

What is terribly missing is the experience of "body life"—that warm fellowship of Christian with Christian which the New Testament calls *koinonia*, and which was an essential part of early Christianity. The New Testament lays heavy emphasis upon the need for Christians to know each other closely and intimately enough to be able to bear one another's burdens, confess faults one to another, rebuke, exhort, and admonish one another, minister to one another with the word and through song and prayer, and thus come to comprehend *with all saints,* as Paul puts it, *what is the breadth and length and height and depth, and to know the love of Christ, which surpasses knowledge* (Eph. 3:18, 19).

Where in the usual traditional church structure of meetings is this kind of interchange possible? What provision is made by church leaders to encourage it and guide its expression through scriptural teaching and wise admonitions? Some expression of it has occurred in private gatherings of Christians, usually in someone's home, but all too often this has been discouraged by church leaders as "divisive," or at least viewed as a threat to the unity of the church.

But in the early church a kind of rhythm of life was evident in which the Christians would gather together in homes to instruct one another, study and pray together, and share the ministry of spiritual gifts. Then they would go out into the world again to let the warmth and glow of their love-filled lives overflow into a spontaneous Christian witness that drew love-starved pagans like a candy store draws little children. This was exactly in line with the exhortation of Jesus to his disciples:

A new commandment I give to you, that you love one another; even as I have loved you, that you also love one another. By this all men will know that you are disciples, if you have love for one another (John 13:34-35).

The early church thus relied upon a twofold witness as the means of reaching and impressing a cynical and unbelieving world: *kerygma* (proclamation) and *koinonia* (fellowship). It was the combination of these two which made their witness so powerful and effective. "In the mouth of two or three witnesses shall every word be established." Pagans could easily shrug off the proclamation as simply another "teaching" among many, but they found it much more difficult to reject the evidence of *koinonia.* The concern of Christians for each other and their evident awareness of sharing life in the same great family of God as brothers and sisters left the pagan world drooling with envy. It prompted the much-quoted remark of a pagan writer: "How these Christians love one another!"

The present-day church has managed to do away with *koinonia* almost completely, reducing the witness of the church to proclamation (*kerygma*) alone. It has thus succeeded in doing two things simultaneously: removing the major safeguard to the health of the church from within, and greatly weakening its effective witness before the world without. It is little wonder, therefore, that the church has fallen on evil days and is regarded as irrelevant and useless by so many in the world.

It is time to take seriously again certain admonitions of Scripture which have somehow been passed over lightly even by so-called Bible-believing Christians. Take, for instance, this strong word from Galatians 6:2: *Bear one another's burdens, and so fulfil the law of Christ.* Note that the apostle indicates that this is the way by which the fundamental law of the Christian life is fulfilled. That law is the word of Jesus, quoted above: *A new commandment I give to you ... that you also love one another* (John 13:34). The law of love is fulfilled only by bearing one another's burdens. But how can Christians bear each other's burdens if they don't know what they are? Some way of sharing these burdens with others is obviously called for. It calls for honesty and openness with other Christians, and a mutual recognition that it is neither abnormal nor unspiritual to have burdens and problems in one's Christian experience. Somehow the masks have to come off, and the facades that say "everything-is-all-right" when everything is anything but right have to be removed. Often this can be done best in small groups, meeting in homes, though it may surprise many to discover how much larger meetings of Christians can be characterized by such a spirit of loving, nonjudgmental acceptance, that many deeply personal problems can be shared openly without fear of rejection or giving rise to scandal. (Chapter twelve will describe just such a meeting, which often involves over a thousand people.)

Now read chapter 9 of *How to Be a People Helper.*

PERSONAL EXERCISES

How do you get along with people in the body of Christ? The answer to this question will in some ways be a good indication of your ability and potential as both a discipleship counselor and a people helper.

1. Give an honest answer, now, to each of the following questions.

    (a) Have you personally invited Christ to be Savior and Lord of your life, thus admitting you to the body of believers? _____

    (b) Are you actively involved in close contact with a group of Christians, preferably in a local church? _____

    (c) Are you interested in building up and improving the quality of your church?
    _____

    (d) Are you really concerned about the needs of other people in your church?
    _____

    (e) Do you know of any specific needs among people in the body? _____
    _____

    (f) Do you recognize and show respect for the unique gifts and abilities of individual believers that you know? _____

    (g) Are you more concerned about *giving* to others in the church or *getting* something from the church for yourself? _____
    _____

If you answered no to any of the first six questions, it is probable that you are not fitting into the body as you should. Hopefully your answer to question (g) is "both."

2. Turn back now to chapter 9 of *How to Be a People Helper*, and skim the section titled "Obstacles to Helping."

3. Most Christians probably have some dissatisfactions with the local church. What sorts of things do you dislike about the church and what do you like? List these below.

Dislikes	*Likes*
(a) _____	(a) _____
(b) _____	(b) _____
(c) _____	(c) _____
(d) _____	(d) _____

Dislikes	*Likes*
(e) _____	(e) _____
(f) _____	(f) _____
(g) _____	(g) _____

(h) _____   (h) _____

(i) _____   (i) _____

(j) _____   (j) _____

4. Now look back over the above. Based on your reactions to these brief exercises, give some serious thought to what you might do to change your attitudes toward the church, what behaviors might change (so that you act differently). In answering, remember what you learned in the Bible study. The spaces below should give your personal plan for being a more effective people helper within the body of Christ.

_____ (a) _____

_____ (b) _____

_____ (c) _____

_____ (d) _____

_____ (e) _____

_____ (f) _____

_____ (g) _____

_____ (h) _____

_____ (i) _____

_____ (j) _____

Looking back over the above list, decide which of these things you should start working on first. Write a number 1 next to this item. Now choose a second and third priority. Start working on number 1 immediately. What will you do first?

_____

_____

_____

_____

If you accomplish the goals listed above, how will this make you a better people helper?

_____

_____

_____

_____

MEETING TOGETHER

In this session we will begin by discussing your answer to numbers 3 and 4 of the above exercises. If the group is large you may want to divide into smaller groups, perhaps your role-play groups.

After about 20 to 25 minutes, listen to the tape (eleven minutes). You may want to take some notes in the space below.

_____

_____

_____

_____

_____

_____

_____

DISCUSSION QUESTIONS

1. In what specific ways can the body of believers help you to be a better people helper?
2. Can you distinguish between interpersonal and relational theology? What are the strengths and weaknesses of each? How does this discussion apply to your activities as a people helper?
3. A recent writer has suggested that "as non-Christians see us, and as they inspect the kind of fellowship we have with one another, they ought to see there a reflection of the Lord whom we serve." Do you agree? What has this got to do with people helping?

WHERE DO WE GO FROM HERE?

Many of us take the local church for granted and sometimes prefer to ignore or criticize it. In this unit we have tried to show how a body of believers can be an important and necessary "backup" for our people helping work. At this point and during the next two units we need to be thinking about how our individual people helping efforts can be carried out with the support and encouragement of other believers.

EXTRA ASSIGNMENT

Body Life, the book by Ray C. Stedman to which we have made previous reference, is worth reading in its entirety (Ventura, California: Regal Books, 1972). The book is available in a paperback edition, and a discussion guide is available from the publisher.

If you wish to learn more about relational (interpersonal) theology, see the excellent article on this subject by Bernard Ramm in the December 1972 issue of *Eternity* magazine. Eternity Book Service, 1716 Spruce Street, Philadelphia, PA 19103 will send you a copy of this article for 25 cents.

11
CAN YOU HELP YOURSELF?

It isn't easy to cope with the problems of life. That is one reason why we need people helpers who can assist one another whenever difficulties arise. When the stresses of living are especially intense or when our problems are deep and complex, it is almost always necessary for us to seek help from a friend, a pastor, or a professional counselor.

But there are times when we can deal with problems pretty much on our own, without the help of someone else. It is to this topic of self-help that we turn in this unit.

GETTING STARTED BY LOOKING TO THE BIBLE

The Scriptures indicate that individuals have a great deal of responsibility for facing and doing something about their own problems. Becoming a Christian is one example. Others may witness about Christ as the Holy Spirit convicts us of sin (John 16:8), but each of us must decide alone whether or not to invite Jesus Christ to be Savior and Lord of our life.

Another example of doing something to help ourselves is recorded in Ephesians 5.

The first verse instructs us to be _____ of God. This is a very high standard, but verses 2-21 give specific directions concerning how this can be done. These instructions center around the word "walk," a word which in the Bible refers to our whole way of living. There are five guidelines given for Christian living. If we follow these guidelines we have a blueprint for meeting our problems.

1. *Walk in love* (read verse 2). If you turn to John 13:35 you will see that love is a major (some would say *the* major) characteristic of a disciple of Jesus Christ. But what does it mean to love? It means to follow the example of Jesus, who showed His love by _____ Himself to others (Ephesians 5:2, 25).

Can the developing of a giving love help the one who is showing the love? _____

How? _____

2. **Walk in purity** (read Ephesians 5:3-7). Verses 3 and 4 list several specific acts or habits that we should avoid. What are these?_____

_____

Notice in verses 5, 6, and 7 that God does not take immorality lightly. How does the avoidance of immorality help us as individuals?_____

_____

3. **Walk in light** (read verses 8-14). Does John 8:12 have any relevance here? _____

_____

Verses 10 and 11 of Ephesians 5 list three activities of those who walk in the light.

(a) _____

(b) _____

(c) _____

In his comments on this passage, William Barclay has written the following:

> . . . In the east the shops in the bazaars are simply little covered enclosures with no windows. Often a man might wish to buy a piece of silk or an article of beaten brass. Before he bought it he would take it out to the street and hold it up to the sun, that the light might reveal any flaws which happened to be in it. He would only purchase it if it stood the test of the light. It is the Christian's duty to expose every action, every decision, every motive to the light of Christ. It is in that light that we must judge everything in life.

How does walking in the light help the walker? _____

_____

4. **Walk in wisdom** (read Ephesians 5:15-17). Here the emphasis is on a wise way of living. "Wise" here means "careful" (like a motorist driving carefully or wisely). Also implied (verse 16) is the idea that we should make the best use of our time, being alert to every opportunity for doing good.

How can being careful and making good use of our time help us? _____

_____

_____

Ephesians 5:17 in the *New American Standard Bible* adds that the wise person understands "what the will of the Lord is." How do we do this? _____

_____

How does this help us? _____

_____

5. **Walk in the spirit** (read Ephesians 5:18-21). Many people today, including many who

want to be people helpers, live lives that are empty and meaningless. They fill the void with so-called pleasures, such as alcohol. But notice that a better alternative is given here. We should be filled with the Spirit.

Bill Bright, president of Campus Crusade for Christ, talks about spiritual breathing by which we exhale sin (by honest confession to God, 1 John 1:9) and inhale the Holy Spirit (by daily asking and expecting that God's Spirit will fill us up).

What does this do for us? Ephesians 5:19 gives an answer which you might write here:

_____

_____

What will be our response if we help ourselves by walking according to these Biblical

guidelines (see verses 20 and 21)? _____

_____

READING

Read the following excerpt adapted with permission from Tim LaHaye's book *Transformed Temperaments* (Wheaton: Tyndale House, 1973) and dealing with how we can walk in the Spirit.

Although I had been in the ministry for a number of years, hostility had been my way of life for thirty-six years. I sincerely wanted to be a servant of God, and I always asked for the Holy Spirit's cleansing and filling just prior to preaching, but I thought that controlling my anger was the same as victory over anger.

Nothing could be further from the truth. One day, at my wife's invitation, I went to Forest Home Conference Grounds to hear Dr. Henry Brandt. I arrived just in time to hear him tell the story of an angry young minister who had come to him for counseling. It was another man, but my story! When he finished his message with Ephesians 4:30-32, I was stunned. Never had I confronted the fact that anger, hostility, and bitterness comprised an awful sin that grieved the Holy Spirit. Quietly I slunk away among the trees and poured out my heart to God. Through his mercy I was cleansed and came away a transformed man.

Facing my anger and hostility was a giant step toward true victory in my life. For the first time I really knew what it was to be filled with the Holy Spirit. Realizing the terrible nature of the sin of anger was a very humbling experience, and I was emotionally subdued for the first time in decades.

The secret of a transformed temperament is the filling of the Holy Spirit, not just on a single occasion, but on a continual basis. Much dis-couragement has assailed believers who erroneously thought that the filling of the Spirit was a once-for-all experience, but Ephesians 5:18 commands us to be continually refilled with the Spirit. A literal translation would read, "And be not drunk with wine, wherein is excess, but be ye being filled with the Spirit." That is, be ye continually in the action of being filled with the spirit. This parallels the admonition in Galatians 5:16: "This I say, then, walk in the Spirit and ye shall not fulfill the lusts of the flesh." Obedience to the flesh is an external indication that we are not internally filled with the Spirit. The cure for overcoming the flesh is "walking in the Spirit."

The first requirement of "walking in the Spirit," of course, is to be filled with the Holy Spirit. I would like to give four simple steps to being filled with the Holy Spirit:

1. *Examine yourself and confess all known sin* (1 John 1:9). If you find that you are not glorifying Jesus, if you do not have power to witness, or if you lack a joyful, submissive spirit or the nine temperament traits of the Holy Spirit, then your self-examination will reveal those areas in which you are deficient and will uncover the sin that causes them. The moment you recognize these deficiencies as sin and confess them to God, He will "cleanse us from all unrighteousness." Until we have done this we cannot have the filling of the Holy Spirit, for He fills only clean vessels. (2 Tim. 2:21).

2. *Submit yourself completely to God* (Rom. 6:11-13). If there is anything in your life that you are unwilling to do or to be, then you are resisting God, and this always limits God's Spirit!

3. *Ask to be filled with the Holy Spirit* (Luke 11:13). Any suggestion to present-day believers of waiting or laboring is man's suggestion. Only the disciples were told to wait, and that was because the day of Pentecost had not yet come.

4. *Believe you are filled and thank Him for it.* If you have followed the first three steps, don't wait for feelings, but fasten your faith to the Word of God that is independent of feeling. Feelings of assurance of the Spirit's filling often follow our taking God at His Word and believing He has filled us.

One of the reasons some Christians are reluctant to think they are filled with the Spirit is that they don't see an immediate change in their lives, or the change is of short duration. Two factors have an important bearing on this: temperament and habit, and they work together. The weaknesses of our temperament have created strong habits which involuntarily recur.

For example, about two hours after my experience at Forest Home, that wonderful feeling of peace and oneness with God drowned in the tidal waves of my habitual hostility.

One of my pet "gripes" in life was the character who suddenly cut me off on the freeway. Many a bitter, hateful word had shot from my tongue in response to such careless driving. It happened again later.

There, while traveling at sixty-five miles per hour on the freeway toward San Diego, I encountered another life-changing experience. While glaring at the offending driver, I suddenly became aware that my peace with God had vanished. Right then, I decided the driver would not cause my spiritual failure. While reducing my speed to avoid a collision, I silently prayed, "Lord, I did it again; please forgive me and take this habit away." Gradually the peace came back.

Yes, there have been other times and other failures, but whenever I confess my anger God in His grace forgives. Now it is almost a thing of the past. Recently, while thinking about the old reactions, I found myself chuckling after being cut off the freeway by a little red sports car. I wouldn't trade my present peace and joy for the old anger and misery under any circumstances.

Many books have been written on how to be filled with the Spirit, but most have not given sufficient emphasis to the fact that being filled with the Spirit is just the beginning of Christian victory. From that point on we must "walk in the Spirit" to be lastingly effective (Gal. 5:16). Since it is a command of God, we must not search for a hard or complex procedure, for God is straightening out our lives, not tangling them up. The following procedure for walking in the Spirit can be a practical tool for victorious daily living.

1. *Make the filling of the Holy Spirit a daily priority.* You cannot walk in the Spirit unless you sincerely want to and unless you have His filling. Only when we consciously and subconsciously want the filling of the Holy Spirit more than anything else in the world are we willing to give up our lesser emotional satisfactions of lust, worry, self-pity, and anger.

I confess that even after several years of experiencing the Holy Spirit's filling, I find that anger is fun. Under certain circumstances, such as when I feel my "rights have been violated," I can anticipate a satisfying bout with anger. However, the Spirit's reminder of the high price I must pay for indulging such an emotion cools me off immediately. No cause for anger is worth the loss of that blessed consciousness of His presence. Gradually the reaction becomes subconscious so that you can begin to say with Paul, "The things I once loved I now hate."

2. *Develop a keen sensitivity to sin.* As we have already seen, sin short-circuits the power of the Holy Spirit in us. The moment we are conscious of any sins of the mind, we should confess them immediately; in this way the time between grieving or quenching the Spirit and reinstatement is minimal.

3. *Daily read and study God's Word.* It is my conviction after a good deal of observation that it is impossible for a Christian to "walk in the Spirit" unless he develops the habit of regularly feeding his mind and heart upon the Word of God. One of the reasons Christians do not "feel" as God does about life issues is that they do not know God's way from his Word. If we feed our minds on the Word of God, we will feel as the Spirit does about life issues. Remember that it takes some time to reorient our minds from human wisdom to divine wisdom. So regular reading is essential. It takes self-discipline to develop good habits of thinking, but once established they become "second nature."

A young engineer came to me after eleven years as a Christian and confessed he had never led a person to Christ. Moreover, he claimed: "I never get an opportunity to witness my faith." But after three months of a consistent Bible reading and memorization program, he told me with a big smile: "That was nonsense about never having an opportunity to witness. I witness all the time now. I previously knew so little about the Bible that I didn't have anything to say, but now that I'm so full of the Word it comes out in almost every conversation!"

A careful comparison of the Spirit-filled life described in Ephesians 5:18-21 with the Word-filled life in Colossians 3:15-17 reveals both passages promise a song in your heart, a thanksgiving attitude, and a submissive spirit. A mind that is filled with and yielded to the Word of God will produce the same effects on our emotions as the mind filled with and yielded to the Holy Spirit. We may legitimately conclude from this that the filling of the Spirit and walking in the Spirit depend upon our filling with the Word of God!

4. *Guard against grieving the Holy Spirit.* The next step for walking in the Spirit is an extension of step two—developing a sensitivity to sin. Ephesians 4:30-32 makes it clear that all forms of hostility, including anger, bitterness, and enmity, grieve the Holy Spirit. All anger-prone believers should memorize those three verses and develop a particular sensitivity to hostility. In addition to making instant confession, they should resolve to be loving, kind, tenderhearted, and forgiving toward others.

This supernaturally induced love is mentally and emotionally healthful as well as spiritually rejuvenating. I counseled two strongwilled men who were maliciously persecuted by their employers. One was fired after he refused to quit under pressure. His Spirit-filled reaction was to lead his family in praying for his employer. This earned him the special admiration of his wife, children, and friends, and he found another job where he contentedly awaits God's further will for his life.

The second man suffered an emotional breakdown from the stress and came to see me a few days after he was released from the psychiatric department of a local hospital. Never had I seen more vehement hatred. The selfishness and brutality of the former employer was still fresh to him, and he would not forgive the offender.

If only he realized the high cost of harboring such hatred, he would forgive the man. Since he grieved the Spirit long ago, he knows nothing about the Spirit-filled life and his hostility is destroying him. Functioning on his own, his mind is playing tricks on him. He is imagining that his wife is unfaithful and his children don't love him. More recently he concluded that even his parents do not love him. All of this abnormal behavior is the perfectly natural result of long-harbored hatred. Christians are admonished to "forgive one another," not only for God's glory and the offender's good, but for the offended one's peace of mind. When you prize the filling of the Holy

Spirit above everything else, you won't let anger, animosity, or unforgiveness grieve the Holy Spirit. You know you can't afford it!

Several years ago I counseled with a couple who had been separated because of the husband's infidelity. He finally repented toward God and his wife and she decided to take him back. Their home was reestablished on a spiritual foundation, but within a month the wife was back in my office in tears. "I hate my husband and can't bear to have him touch me!" she sobbed. Prior to his unfaithfulness she had dearly loved him, I knew. After asking God for wisdom, I inquired if she had forgiven her husband for what he had done. She sat up straight and fire blazed in her eyes. "Why should I? He doesn't deserve to be forgiven! As a Christian he knew better than that!"

All of this was true, of course. As gently as possible I showed her that none of us deserves forgiveness, yet God commands us to forgive one another even as he forgives us. When she realized she didn't want to forgive her husband and this grieved the Holy Spirit, she began to pray. Forgetting her husband's sin, she began to concentrate on her own sins of resentment, hatred, and lack of forgiveness. She got up from her knees a transformed woman. Today she is a Spirit-filled, radiant Christian who joyfully loves her husband—certainly a rich reward for obediently forgiving one who didn't deserve forgiveness!

The importance of our will becomes apparent at this point of walking in the Spirit. When we feel the bludgeon of injustice or someone's wrath, we are forced either to hate the offender or to forgive and pray for him. Our overall feelings as well as our walk in the Spirit depend upon our decision. Don't be surprised if you fail repeatedly at first. Only be sure that you confess the sin as soon as you are aware of grieving the Spirit, and let him reestablish your walk. As you choose to forgive and to let the Holy Spirit react with patience and love, you will find your temperament weakness changing into a strength.

5. *Avoid quenching the Spirit through fear and worry.* According to 1 Thessalonians 5:16-19, we quench the Holy Spirit when we doubt and resist His dealings in our lives. When a Christian says, "I don't understand why God let this awful thing happen to me," he has already quenched the Spirit through fear and is no longer walking in the Spirit. The Christian who is trusting God could face the same circumstances and say, "I thank God He is in control of my life! I don't understand His dealings with me right now, but I trust His promise that He will never leave me

and He will supply my every need." Such a Christian continues to walk in the Spirit and "feels good" in spite of adverse circumstances.

We have seen that melancholy and phlegmatic people have a predisposition toward fear, just as the more extrovertive temperaments have a predisposition toward anger. Some people possess both introvertive and extrovertive temperaments, and consequently may have deep problems with both fear and anger. God's grace is sufficient to cure both problems through His Holy Spirit. But if you have these tendencies, you need to watch carefully your reaction to seemingly unfavorable events. You need to be willing to call your doubt-induced complaining exactly what it is—sin—and ask God to transform this habit pattern and fill you with His Spirit.

Frequently I meet people who say, "I tried that, but it didn't work." What they may have tried is to escape an undesirable problem or difficulty through confession of their complaining, rather than accepting the *problem* and thanking God for it. God is not nearly so interested in changing circumstances as he is in changing people.

It is impossible for a fear-prone Christian to walk in the Spirit any length of time without strong infusions of God's Word to encourage his faith. The more God's Word fills his mind, the more his feelings abound in faith. But worriers usually enjoy wallowing in their misery, especially with God watching the piteous scene. Prayer for such people often makes them feel worse. As they whine in prayer, they stamp their misfortunes more deeply on their minds and feel worse at the end of their prayer than when they started. That does not mean prayer is bad; it means the wrong kind of prayer is bad. We must go to God's Word to see what constitutes beneficial prayer.

All worriers should memorize Philippians 4:6-7: "Be careful for nothing; but in everything by prayer and supplication with thanksgiving let your requests be made known unto God. And the peace of God, which passeth all understanding, shall keep your hearts and minds through Christ Jesus." These verses direct prayer to be made "with thanksgiving." You cannot genuinely pray with thanksgiving and finish with the same burdens you started with.

If you tend to worry or grumble, you will find that you are not a very thankful person. The secret to a thanksgiving attitude is in coming to know God intimately as He reveals Himself in His Word. This will require consistent Bible reading, studying, and meditation. When your faith is established through the Word, it is easier

to give thanks, but it is still an act of the will. If you have not accepted the Lord's full leading for your life, you will complain because you doubt things will turn out all right. And doubt quenches the Spirit and sidetracks your real progress.

Several months ago I experienced the most devastating emotional trauma that had entered my life since my father died thirty-four years ago. For almost three years I had worked on a project desperately needed by our church—new property. After much prayer and work, our people caught the vision to trust God for the impossible. We purchased forty-three acres of ground near two freeways at an approximate cost of $500,000. We considered it the most strategic location in our city for a growing church.

Somehow local politics got involved, and some of the city fathers began to oppose the zone change we needed to build on our property. For two years we carried on a running battle with city hall. We spent thousands of dollars on lawyers' and engineers' fees plus an equal number of man-hours. Through all that time there was absolutely no doubt in my mind that the plans would be approved and we would build a beautiful church to God's glory. Then on October 7, 1969, after hours of deliberation, the city council voted six to two *against* us. I was so stunned I couldn't get up out of my chair at first. Eventually I mustered enough strength to leave as discreetly as possible.

When I finally got away from everyone, I drove alone to the property. I didn't have the courage to visit the spot where my wife and I had knelt and claimed that property for God. Instead, I went out to a lovely vantage point and sat down in the dirt to think. Can you imagine the nature of my first thoughts? "Why, Lord? I prayed over this place, I walked over it and claimed it, just as others did for theirs. Why did you let a selfish politician who didn't want a church next to his house disgrace your good name and that of our church?"

And the more I griped, the worse I felt. About that time the opposing politician drove into his driveway. I watched from my spot of self-pity across the canyon from his house as he got out of his big Lincoln Continental and presented his wife with a basket of flowers to celebrate his victory. Guess how I felt! Absolutely miserable.

For two days I went through the worst siege of depression I have ever experienced. Finally it dawned on me that I had quenched the Holy Spirit and was walking in a very carnal state. After confessing my sins of self-pity, doubt, griping, and questioning God, I began thanking

Him. I thanked him for His power and leading, and that though I didn't know what He was going to do, the problem wasn't really mine but His.

A thrilling thing happened that day. The depression lifted, my spirit began to rise, and a deep peace flooded my heart. During succeeding months, though actively engaged in the search for new property and knocking on every door of opportunity, I gained no more idea of God's plan for our church than I had had on October 7. The thrilling part, however, is that I have not felt the slightest twinge of discouragement. Our people have responded in such faith that we are convinced God has something better for us than we had planned before. Only God can produce joy and peace in the face of seeming chaos.

This valuable lesson points out that there are two kinds of thanks. The first kind is natural and easy when we are walking by sight: we know where we are going and the prospects are pleasant. The second is supernatural and is by faith: we cannot see what God is doing or why, but we are thankful He is leading, and He will never forsake us. That kind of thanksgiving comes while walking in the Spirit.

One last practical suggestion for walking in the Spirit is in order here. Although mental attitude is important at all times, it is of paramount importance twice during each day: when we go to bed, and when we arise. It is very important to pray "with thanksgiving" and "in everything give thanks" as well as reading the Scriptures at night. Though it may be hard, the other strategic time to give thanks is the first thing in the morning.

After beginning your day with thanksgiving, yield yourself anew to God according to Romans 6:11-13. Tell Him you are available to share your faith with the needy one He sends to you. Yield your lips to the Holy Spirit and let him open the conversation. Walk in the spirit and you will bear fruit for God. As soon as you sense you have grieved or quenched the Spirit, confess your sin and again ask for His filling. If you follow these steps, you temperament will truly be transformed!

Now read chapter 10 of *How to Be a People Helper*.

PERSONAL EXERCISES

In counseling classes, students are often asked to write a brief personal autobiography on the assumption that a good way to help yourself is to know about yourself. In the next three pages, write an autobiography, using the guidelines as suggested.

1. What are your significant life events (including people who have had an important influence on your life)?

2. Who are the significant people in your life? How do you relate to them?

3. Summarize your strengths and weaknesses, personal problems, and concerns (including a statement of what you are doing or plan to do in order to improve).

4. State your helping effectiveness (including a summary statement of what there is about you that will enable you to be a good helper and what might hinder your helping effectiveness).

5. Summarize your future plans.

6. Describe other pertinent information about yourself.

MEETING TOGETHER

We will begin this session with a tape. Take notes in the space below.

_____

_____

_____

_____

_____

_____

_____

_____

Following the tape, divide into small role-play groups. Each member of the group should share his or her autobiography with the other group members. Keep track of the time, so that every member has opportunity to share.

DISCUSSION QUESTIONS

1. What are the main values to be gained from writing and discussing an autobiography? Are there weaknesses with this exercise?

2. Helping, it has been suggested, consists largely of education. Do you agree? When do we help without educating?

3. The chapter in *How to Be a People Helper* lists ten ways to help yourself. What are these? Do you agree with the author's suggestions? Can you think of other things which should be added or eliminated?

4. Does walking as an "imitator of God" really help with our problems, as the Bible study suggests?

WHERE DO WE GO FROM HERE?

It is difficult (although not impossible) to be helpful to others when we are bogged down with our own problems. This unit should stimulate you to evaluate where you stand physically, psychologically, and spiritually. If changes are needed, now is the time to begin. In the long run, you will feel better, function more efficiently, and be a better people helper.

EXTRA ASSIGNMENT

You might want to read portions or all of the author's book *Overcoming Anxiety* (Ventura, California: Vision House, 1973). The book discusses ways in which we can deal with such issues as anxiety, discouragement, guilt, loneliness, inferiority, and other common problems.

12
WHERE
DO YOU GO
FROM HERE?

We come now to the end of our people helper program. Hopefully these sessions together have helped you to develop sensitivity and skills which will, in turn, enable you to help others. In this last unit we will try to consolidate our learning and think together about how we can apply what we have learned in our people helping activities.

GETTING STARTED BY LOOKING TO THE BIBLE

At various times throughout this program we have emphasized the importance of discipleship. Let us go back to this theme by turning to Matthew 28 and re-reading verses 18-20.

Throughout His adult ministry, Jesus was actively involved in making disciples. Near the start of this process, He met with the twelve on a mountain and outlined what they needed to know as disciples. Time does not permit us to study all of this Sermon on the Mount, but we might look at the first part, Matthew 5:1-16, from the point of view of discipleship and people helping.

1. *The Characteristics of Discipleship*

The "beatitudes" is the name given to the several verses which begin with "blessed are . . . ." These are traits which should characterize the real disciple of Christ. In each case we will look at (1) the trait, (2) the promise that comes to those who develop the trait, and (3) the relevance of this trait for people helping. "Blessed are . . ." might be translated "Oh the joy of . . . ."

(a) *Verse 3.* (1) Oh the joy of _____ . Here are people who recognize their real lack of resources for meeting life.

　　(2) To them comes _____ . When a person recognizes his or her helplessness, there is a dependence on God which brings a real spiritual richness as a citizen of the kingdom of heaven.

(3) Relevance for people helping? _____

_____ .

(b) *Verse 4.* (1) Oh the joy of _____ . Here
is a sincere sorrow over the world's sin and needs.

    (2) To them comes _____ . This includes
sincere joy.

    (3) Relevance for people helping? _____

_____ .

(c) *Verse 5.* (1) Oh the joy of _____ . Meekness
is not a namby-pamby attitude. According to one writer, meekness refers to the person
"who is always angry at the right time and never angry at the wrong time, who has
every instinct and impulse and passion under control because he or she is God-
controlled." Meekness also implies humility and gentleness.

    (2) To them comes_____ . These people
are kings and queens among their fellow human beings.

    (3) Relevance for people helping? _____

_____ .

(d) *Verse 6.* Oh the joy of _____ . Here are
people who want desperately to be holy and godly.

    (2) To them comes_____ .

    (3) Relevance for people helping? _____

_____ .

(e) *Verse 7.* (1) Oh the joy of _____ .

    (2) To them comes_____ . William
Barclay gives a thought-provoking paraphrase of this verse which has real relevance for
people helping:

Oh the bliss of the man who gets right inside other people, until he can see with their eyes,
think with their thoughts, feel with their feelings, for he who does that will find others do the
same for him, and will know that that is what God in Jesus Christ has done!

    (3) Relevance for people helping? _____

_____ .

(f) *Verse 8.* (1) Oh the joy of _____ . This
concerns our motives. The pure in heart have pure, unselfish motives.

    (2) To them comes_____ . What do
you think of that promise? Does it refer to the present, the future, or both?

    (3) Relevance for people helping? _____

_____ .

(g) *Verse 9.* (1) Oh the joy of _____ . Notice
that this does not say "peace-lovers" or "peace-keepers."

(2) To them comes_____. Barclay writes this about verse 9: "Blessed are the peace-makers, for they shall be doing a God-like work. The man who makes peace is engaged in the very work which the God of peace is doing (Romans 15:33; 2 Corinthians 13:11; 1 Thessalonians 5:23; Hebrews 13:20)." Thus such a person is a "son of God," doing a God-like work.

(3) Relevance for people helping? _____

_____ .

2. *The Evidence of Discipleship*

The beatitudes set a high standard for the disciple-people helper. It appears that as we approach such a standard there will be three obvious results:

(a) *Persecution* (read Matthew 5:10-12). Why are disciples persecuted?_____

_____ .

What should be the response of the persecuted? _____ .

(b) *Penetration* (read verse 13). Salt stops decay, purifies, and adds flavor. The disciple-people helper does all three as he or she interacts with others.

(c) *Illumination* (read verses 14-16). Light is very visible. There is no such thing as invisible, secret discipleship. Look carefully at verse 16. The true disciple does good works but directs the glory to God.

READING

The following excerpt is taken from the author's book *A Psychologist Looks at Life*. This book has been reprinted under the title *Overcoming Anxiety* (Ventura, California: Vision House, 1973), but the following excerpt is not included in the *Overcoming Anxiety* book.

Why should people get discouraged, angry, or envious? What causes men and women to feel emptiness, loneliness, or guilt? Why do some people feel inferior while others are so proud? Why are some of us bored with life while others run around in hectic activity, excitement, and busyness?

It may have occurred to you that some people are more bothered by these problems than are others. Some of us are better able to handle the stresses and emotions of life. Some people appear to be very flexible and able to cope quickly, while others are more rigid, inflexible, and unable to adapt so readily. This rigidity or inflexibility is the problem to which we turn in this last chapter.

Our ability to adapt to new situations determines in large measure how we can handle or deal with the challenges of life. The more flexible we are, the fewer our problems, and the more successful are we in coping with stress.

Rigidity and flexibility have always been important issues, but they are especially crucial in our day. The society in which we live is changing drastically, and we must move with the times or risk being left behind feeling discouraged, unhappy, irrelevant, and maladjusted. Rigidity and adaptability, therefore, are issues that fall not only on individuals but on whole societies, governments, educational institutions, and churches.

Characteristics of Modern Man

What is modern man really like? In the first place, it appears that he is *dissatisfied*. He is distressed over pollution, incessant warfare, injustice in the ghettos, crime in the streets, laxity in the courts, hypocrisy in the business world, corruption in the government, irresponsibility in the young, self-satisfaction in the old, and deadness in the church. Young people are most vocal in expressing these dissatisfactions but they are not the only ones bothered. Even those in the over-thirty generation, if we can be honest, realize that our society is plagued by a host of social ills that are leading to widespread anxiety, despair, and frustration.

We should recall, however, that dissatisfaction is nothing new. Adam and Eve were dissatisfied with the way God organized the Garden of Eden—ever since then people have been dissatisfied. Those who want to preserve the status quo and those who want to change it are both frustrated and unwilling to sit and do nothing. This brings us to a second characteristic of modern man. Because of his dissatisfaction, he is *protesting*.

When people are dissatisfied and frustrated because nothing seems to be getting better, they often begin to shout and shove. Marches, civil disobedience, riots, destruction, and violence are all contributing to make this an age of protest. While many people rightly condemn the illegal behavior of some protestors, things are not likely to change in the immediate future—primarily because protests work. They bring about change and enable dissatisfied people to get what they want and to get it quickly.

It would be easy and more comfortable to dismiss such protests as the irresponsible and enthusiastic actions of a few immature and overly pampered young people, but the protests are much more widespread. Thousands of dissatisfied people, including many who are older, are dedicated to the making of "a culture so radically disaffiliated from the mainstream assumptions of our society that it scarcely looks to many as a culture at all, but takes on the alarming appearance of a barbaric intrusion."

This leads to the third characteristic of man: he is *revolutionary*. A revolution can be defined as the taking of a situation that has proved to be unworkable, old fashioned, archaic, impractical, or out-of-date; tearing it down; and replacing it with a system that works. This is not always bad—some revolutions are bloodless and bring many worthwhile changes—but the word revolution as used today usually refers to something violent and destructive.

It means bloodshed, rioting, rebellion, anarchy, and insurrection. Jerry Rubin, leader of the Yippies and one of the notorious "Chicago seven" who were charged with conspiracy to overthrow the government, once wrote a book entitled *Do It*. One reviewer has called this volume unspeakably vulgar, absurdly irrational, and deliberately shocking, but the book is a clear and explicit cry for violent revolution. "Act first," Rubin writes, "analyze later. Impulse—not theory—makes the great leaps forward."

It is easy to ignore attention-seeking writing of a radical like Jerry Rubin, but listen to Black evangelist Tom Skinner. In his opinion, "revolution in America is inevitable.... America is at her crisis hour." Evangelist Leighton Ford agrees:

> ... This is the mark of our age—not an isolated revolt, but total revolution. Revolution is change—total, constant, irresistible, rapid, pervasive change—which affects every part of our lives....

Revolution also means radical political change. A few years ago that prospect seemed remote on this continent. Did you ever think you would live to see a revolution in America? Today, extremist groups in our society call for just that. What the radicals have in mind is not akin to the American Revolution, with its limited goals. Their vision is much closer to the French and Communist revolutions, which totally rejected the old regimes.

They are convinced that American society is so corrupt and so unworkable that the system cannot be changed; it must be destroyed. When asked what they have to replace it, many of them answer that that is not their concern.

In a recent article, Ford. wrote, "Our world is going to have a revolution. Have no doubt about it. The question is which revolution: the revolution of hate and violence or Christ's revolution of love and spiritual power."

The prospect of cataclysmic upheaval is made worse by a fourth characteristic of modern man: he is *antiintellectual*. Several months ago, one of my students was invited to participate in a week-long seminar on theology to be held at a very respectable Midwestern college. In accordance with the letter of invitation, the student prepared a carefully written and logically organized speech in support of Biblically based Christianity. He then arrived at the college only to find that all of the other speakers were from liberal seminaries, that none had bothered to prepare speeches, and that all advocated physical "love-ins" and sensitivity sessions in place of any intellectual discussion of Christianity.

Recently, a Chicago newspaper printed a feature article on new forms of worship. The article described one church service in which glass slides and paint were distributed to members of the congregation, who then painted swirls and crude designs. When these pictures were placed on an opaque projector a nun dropped in clippings from magazine ads with words such as "It's the Real Thing!" "Peace," and "Love." As she described her work to the newspaper reporter, the nun exclaimed, "Who knows? If we do this perhaps a message might be in there somewhere."

This is the plight of modern man. He has thrown out the revealed Word of God and has no solid message on which to build his life. He does not want to think but prefers instead to feel and to have experiences. Thus, promiscuous sex, widespread use of drugs, increased interest in the experiences of Eastern religion, and nude love-in groups are becoming more and more popular. Many believe that there is no absolute truth or standards of right and wrong. Instead, the world is thought to be irrational and illogical, that only experience can remain.

Perhaps it is not surprising that modern man is also *religious*. He is caught up in a variety of religious systems, including mysticism, Zen-Buddhism, Satan worship, occultism, and spiritism. But a void remains. Manmade religions don't work, and for many life still remains a vacuum of unbelief.

This leads to at least one other characteristic of modern man: he is *open*. Men today are open to finding a new cause for living, open to finding a God in whom they can believe, open to finding order in the midst of chaos, open to finding stability in a revolutionary age.

This openness presents the church with one of the greatest opportunities of its history. Jesus Christ is able to meet men's needs, and people today are wide open to the Gospel message. But regretfully many of us in the church are too comfortable, too self-centered, and too rigid to bother sharing the good news.

The Meaning of Rigidity

Rigidity can be defined somewhat formally as the inability or refusal to change one's actions or attitudes, even though objective conditions make change desirable. The rigid person clings to thinking and ways of acting that are no longer appropriate. He resists change and cannot adapt to new ideas and ways of acting.

Rigidity is not something we either have or don't have. Instead, rigidity can be placed on a scale. At one end is complete and perpetual rigidity and at the other end is total flexibility. Most of us are somewhere in between, but some people are closer to the rigid end than are others.

```
|_____|
complete, perpetual                complete, perpetual
     rigidity                          flexibility
```

The Rigidity-Flexibility Scale. Rigidity can be placed on a scale from complete rigidity to complete flexibility. Few people, if any, are at the ends of the scale. Most of us are somewhere in between.

A person's position on this rigidity-flexibility scale depends on at least three factors. The first of these is the specific issue or belief. For several years psychologists tried to design tests that would tell where people were on the rigidity-flexibility scale in general, but it was soon discovered that a person who is rigid about one idea or belief might be quite flexible about something else. When it comes to political beliefs, for example, someone may pride himself on being very flexible and willing to shift back and forth from one political party to another depending on the issue or on the personality of the candidates. In contrast, the same person may be much more rigid when it comes to theological issues.

There are also individual differences in the rigidity with which we view a theological issue like salvation. Some people are flexible. They believe that there are many ways to heaven and that a man can pretty much find his own route. But the Bible is much more rigid on this issue. Jesus said, "I am the way . . . no man comes to the Father but by me." On some issues, therefore, we can and probably should be more flexible, but on others we must be firm and inflexible.

Secondly, one's position on the rigidity-flexibility scale depends on past learning. Sometimes we learn to be rigid thinkers who approach every problem in the same way and are unable to think creatively or differently. Prejudice is an example of this. We learn that a person of another race is supposed to act in a certain way, so this is what we look for and that is what we eventually see. If facts are presented to disprove our prejudices, we dismiss the new information and call it "the exception which proves the rule." Habits are also the result of our learning to be rigid, for what is a habit if it is not a consistent, persistent, and rigid way of acting based on our past learning?

Third, whether or not we are rigid depends upon how secure we feel. When stress comes along or when we face a new situation, some people feel very uncomfortable and insecure. Instead of trying to adapt to the new situation, these people fall back to some kind of behavior that has worked in the past. They feel more comfortable and less threatened if they can rigidly cling to the old ways of doing things and never have to try anything new. Many of the emotions which have been discussed in this book persist because we are too insecure and too rigid to change or try new behavior. A rigid clinging to the status quo has become a defense.

Rigidity, of course, isn't always bad. Often the

old ways do work best and sometimes the old beliefs really are true. But this rigidity can also be harmful. By digging in and refusing to budge, we become more and more detached from our changing society, and we become less and less able to adapt to the demands of twentieth-century living.

The Future Shock

Almost everyone has heard of culture shock. It is a reaction of confusion and disorientation which occurs when a person arrives in a culture that is very different from his own. Missionaries often experience this when they arrive on the foreign field and are temporarily overwhelmed by the strangeness. Foreign students experience this when they arrive to study in another part of the world, and tourists are sometimes surprised and unsure of themselves as they travel in unfamiliar countries. Perhaps this is why one person has described the tourist as "a person who wants to travel someplace which is different and then complains because it is."

In the early 1970's a new book was published which skyrocketed quickly to the top of the best-seller list. It dealt not with culture shock but with "a much more serious malady: future shock." According to the author, culture shock arises as you move from one society to another, but future shock comes when you stay put and watch your own society change before your eyes. Very convincingly the author argues that the world is changing so rapidly people can't keep up. Think, for example, of what has happened in your lifetime and then guess what changes might occur before, say, the year 2000. Little wonder that there is so much anxiety, discouragement, loneliness, inferiority, and uncertainty in our society.

We can't be overwhelmed by all of this change, but neither can we remain rigid in a rapidly accelerating society. Somehow we must cope with the changes, and, according to the writer of *Future Shock*, we must help each other to face the future. We need creative planning for the months and years that are ahead. We must teach people how to be more flexible. We need to think carefully before we try new ways of doing things, recognizing that change and non-change can at times each be bad.

The Christian and Rigidity

What does this have to do with the church and individual Christians who are trying to cope with life? Not long ago Francis Schaeffer, the well-known theologian in Switzerland, published a book entitled *The Church at the End of the 20th Century*. "The evangelical church seems to specialize in being behind," Schaeffer wrote,

> But the major problem we are going to face . . . in the next 30 years is revolution with repression. Society is going to change. I believe that when my grandchildren grow to maturity, they will face a culture that has little similarity to ours. And the church today should be getting ready and talking about issues of tomorrow and not about issues of 20 or 30 years ago . . . . This is not a day for a sleepy church.

The March 12, 1971, issue of *Christianity Today* echoes this sentiment. "Cries of revolution, instead of goading us into fresh initiatives, sometimes intimidate us into quiet retreat. We cower in the corners of our sanctuaries, hoping that the storms of change will pass by to leave us unscathed. This kind of reaction is clearly not that prescribed by the New Testament."

Recently I met with a group of teenagers who were talking about their church and their faith. Christianity doesn't mean much in the lives of our parents, these young people concluded, so why should we get excited about it? Sunday school classes and youth groups are boring and the deacons balk when we suggest anything different. We come here because our parents make us come, but we don't find the church very much geared to the needs of men, women, or teenagers today.

Similar views, I suspect, are held by numerous people of all ages in our Western society. In England, for example, church attendance is exceptionally low, and we in North America are moving in the same direction. The faithful few will keep coming, often because of habit or because they feel guilty and uncomfortable when they miss a service. And many churches—including some evangelical churches—are fizzling out and moving toward death. This terminal illness will only be stopped when we are creative enough, honest enough, and secure enough to keep abreast of the times. We must learn to anticipate what life will be like in the future and to prepare for it instead of dragging our feet.

If people don't attend our services in the evenings, in the summers, or on Wednesdays, we need to ask why. Can we honestly expect that things will get better if we continue as we have in the past, or do we need to think about changing the time of our meetings, the format, or other aspects of our program? If young people are dissatisfied or people in the community are disinterested we must ask why and ponder whether we need to change in some way. If people aren't coming to Christ and Christians aren't growing, there is something wrong in the local church, and the problem may very well be one of stagnation, rigidity, and fear of change in the pastor or congregation. If we are really honest, many of the readers of this book will have to admit that we are dissatisfied with dull meetings and meaningless church activity. We see no signs of improvement in the future and we are afraid to suggest new ways of doing things, but we hang on out of a sense of duty or perhaps because of our rigidity and resistance to change.

Change, of course, isn't always desirable. Sometimes the old ways *are* the best ways, and I am not suggesting a change in our theology. In an age of dissatisfaction, protest, revolution, anti-intellectualism, religiosity, and cataclysmic upheaval, we have a God who doesn't change, a Word that is absolutely reliable and true, a faith that is steadfast and sure, and a Savior who is Lord of all and powerful over the universe. We need this Savior and this message in our lives, and we need to proclaim them to others.

The urgent importance of our being flexible and relevant was emphasized recently by an editorial writer in *Decision* magazine:

Whether we like it or not, the spotlight is upon the evangelical cause today. Many quarters are showing a new interest in spiritual values, in the Bible, in the person of Christ. As people investigate these areas, some are taking a second look at us to see if they missed anything the first time around. It could be our moment on the stage of time. In other words, perhaps the ball has been passed to the evangelicals . . . .

Now, what do we have to offer . . .?

What have we to offer as against the juntas and pills and vacant pews? Let's not argue the point as to whether people are turning to us. Numbers of them *are* turning. What do we do?

Do we slide into the old behavior patterns that made people turn away from us in the first place?

Do we treat Jesus Christ as an orthodox cliche?

Do we fiddle around in the pulpit with things that don't matter a straw to God or man, while neglecting the immortal souls of our neighbors?

Do we talk just about people's souls, to the complete disregard of their total being?

Do we burn up God's time in committee meetings that never should have been called in the first place?

Do we spray ourselves with religious deodorant and hope this will carry us through?

Do we encourage people to look past us to the face of our Lord and Savior, the Prince of Glory?

Do we advise them to receive Jesus Christ, who alone can meet every human need?

Do we tell them how to do it?

Do we stir up a shout in the camp, and make the pulpit a platform for proclaiming the Good News of salvation to the whole world?

What a magnificent thing it would be if those who are taking a second look at us found Jesus Christ instead! Think what it would mean for our world. Let us not fluff this chance. Let us get out of God's way. Let us hunt for people he can reach. Let us look for feet to wash. Let us put on the Lord Jesus Christ, and speak lovingly of him everywhere we go. Let us put on humility, and drink at the Word of Wisdom, and deal in the fruit of the Spirit. If the ball has been passed to us, let's not fumble it.

If we are to keep from fumbling the ball in a time when people are confused about life, we must not be rigid, inflexible, and so unwilling to even consider change that the world passes us by, that our young people give up in disgust, that the gospel is dismissed as an archaic, irrelevant remnant of the past. "I am come," Jesus said, "that you might have life and that you might have it more abundantly." That same Jesus has the power to help us cope with and sometimes completely overcome anxiety, discouragement, anger, guilt, inferiority, pride, envy, loneliness, emptiness, busyness, phoniness, and rigidity. Let us be flexible enough to completely yield to Him. Let us be willing to take up our cross and follow Him. This is what gives a new kind of life in an age of protest, change, and internal turmoil.

PERSONAL EXERCISES

1.   What have you learned in this program which will help you to be a better people helper? Write a brief summary below. What are the implications for your family? Your work? Your service for Christ?

_____

_____

_____

_____

_____

_____

2.   In the first chapter of this book you recorded your reaction to a series of ten statements. Please turn to page 118 and complete the exercise again. When you have finished, compare your responses with those in chapter 1. Have there been any changes? _____ How do you account for any change?

_____

_____

_____

_____

3.   Go back to chapter 2 of *How to be a People Helper* (page 31) and review what is meant by empathy, warmth, and genuineness.
   Now look at the following rating scales:

empathy						
warmth						
genuineness						
overall helping effectiveness	extremely poor	poor	fair	adequate	good	extremely good

Rate yourself by putting a checkmark (✓) where you think you belong on these scales

Now turn to page 120 and rate the other members of your role-play groups.

MEETING TOGETHER

Start this session by breaking down into your role-play groups. Share with each other the ratings from page 120 of this growthbook on the above rating scales. You may want to record the ratings that your fellow group members made of you. Are there discrepancies? How do you account for these differences? (Discuss this in the group.) What characteristics do you need to develop more?

After fifteen or twenty minutes everyone should come together as a group. As a group, discuss the reasons for any changes in the responses to the statements which were evaluated in chapter 1 and in this chapter. Also discuss reasons for the lack of changes. What could be done to bring about more change in the future?

Now listen to the tape. Take notes below.

_____

_____

_____

_____

_____

_____

DISCUSSION QUESTIONS

1. What are some specific, practical ways in which you can apply what you have learned from this growthbook to the needs of people around you? How can this apply to your own family?

2. What is your reaction to the reading assigned to this chapter? Are the six characteristics of modern man—dissatisfied, protesting, revolutionary, anti-intellectual, religious, open—typical of people in your church or community? What would you add or subtract from the list? What is the relevance of this list to people helping?

3. As a group, how would you evaluate this people helper program? How could it be adapted to make it more helpful for you?

WHERE DO WE GO FROM HERE?

It would be easy at this point to close this book and never use what you have learned. Remember, however, that as disciples of Jesus Christ we have a responsibility to bear burdens, to rejoice and weep with others, to witness for Christ, and to teach others. Hopefully, this people helper program will enable you to fulfill these responsibilities more effectively. You can wait for people to contact you, or you can take some initiative in contacting others who are in need. The epilogue gives some suggestions for doing the latter.

EXTRA ASSIGNMENT

You may want to rate yourself and others on characteristics other than the four scales that were included with part 3 of the Personal Exercises section of this chapter. Use such traits as ability to keep confidences, immediacy, sensitivity, concern with spiritual issues, desire to help, listening ability, etc.

If you want to keep abreast of developments in the field of Christian people helping, you may wish to subscribe to the *Journal of Psychology and Theology* (1409 No. Walnut Grove Avenue, Rosemead, California 91770).

EPILOGUE

Having completed the people helper training program (PHTP), it would be logical for you to ask, "What do I do now? Where do I go from here?" This postscript to the book gives some preliminary answers to these questions.

In their book *Helping Skills: A Basic Training Program* (New York: Behavioral Publications, 1973), Steve J. Danish and Allen L. Hauser suggest that there are three requirements for anyone who wants to be an effective people helper: 1) an understanding of yourself; 2) some knowledge of helping skills; and 3) experience in applying these skills. The PHTP has attempted to provide all three of these requirements, but with two additions: 4) an understanding of the Biblical basis for people helping and 5) an emphasis on the importance of discipleship and the Great Commission as a framework for our people helping activities.

Persons who complete the PHTP are often able to find creative ways for implementing their training. In addition to using the skills at home and at one's place of work, some people have found that the training is helpful in working with young people, church staff members, Sunday school students, and church members who are ill or in special need. In addition:

—pastoral counselors can make referrals of parishioners and other counselees (including those who call on the telephone) to graduates of the PHTP;

—some graduates can, in turn, teach the program to youth leaders, church leaders, or others who work with identifiable groups;

—teenagers and college-age young people can be encouraged to use the training in talking to their friends, in working in the church, or in their involvement with coffeehouses or similar ministries;

—discipleship training programs (like those of such organizations as Campus Crusade for Christ, Inter-Varsity Christian Fellowship, Navigators, Campus Life, and Young Life), which train people in evangelism, can follow this training with the PHTP, thereby enabling disciplers to minister more effectively to the spiritual and psychological needs of those being discipled;

—pastors, missionaries, other religious leaders, church members, family members—all can apply the people helper skills to their own lives to increase their effectiveness in relating to people.

When people complete evangelism training programs there is often no planned follow-up program. The graduates of the training ask the Lord to lead them to someone who needs to hear the gospel—and that prayer is invariably answered. Might something similar be possible for PHTP graduates? People all around us need help, and many are praying for assistance. By being open to divine leading, the God of the universe may very well lead you to someone who needs a people helper. People in need of help may cast their burdens on the Lord, who, in turn, may use willing people like you to sustain the needy.

One warning must be added in conclusion. Our task is not to force ourselves on people who may be in need but who don't want our help. People helpers must not be pests. In the words of an old song, our theme should be "I'm available." Such available people can and will be people helpers, fulfilling the Great Commission and bearing one another's burdens as the Scriptures command. May God guide as you put your training into practice.

APPENDIX

ROLE PLAY RATING SCALE

Date_____ Helper _____ Helpee _____

Watch the helper very carefully and check what you observe. If you see something more than once, check it more than once. The space below is for you to jot down notes about what you might have seen in the practice session.

Sitting and Movements

_____ 1. faces helpee squarely
_____ 2. looks at helpee
_____ 3. looks away from helpee

_____ 4. slouches or sits rigidly erect
_____ 5. sits in a relaxed manner
_____ 6. nods head
_____ 7. shows nervous mannerisms
_____ 8. shows distracting gestures
_____ 9. shows helpful gestures
_____ 10. touches the helpee
_____ 11. other_____

Responses

_____ 12. asks yes-no questions
_____ 13. asks more general questions
_____ 14. ask "why?" questions
_____ 15. asks a series of questions without pausing for an answer
_____ 16. asks probing questions (to get more information)
_____ 17. gives reassurance, encourages
_____ 18. expresses understanding
_____ 19. says "mm-hmm"
_____ 20. gives explanations

_____ 21. gives advice
_____ 22. gives moral judgments
_____ 23. responds to helpee feelings
_____ 24. responds to content statements
_____ 25. comments on helpee behavior
_____ 26. is silent
_____ 27. confronts
_____ 28. other_____

Voice

_____ 29. shaky and nervous voice
_____ 30. steady and reassuring voice
_____ 31. voice too loud
_____ 32. voice too soft
_____ 33. other_____

Helper Characteristics

_____ 34. patient
_____ 35. understanding
_____ 36. accepting
_____ 37. shows warmth and empathy
_____ 38. avoids discussing difficult issues
_____ 39. excessively curious
_____ 40. other_____

In general, the following are considered to be helpful and desirable responses: 1, 2, 5, 6, 9, 13, 16, 17, 18, 19, 23, 24, 25, 26, 30, 34, 35, 36, and 37.

_____

Notes:

_____
Name of Observer-Evaluator

ROLE PLAY RATING SCALE

Date_____ Helper _____ Helpee _____

Watch the helper very carefully and check what you observe. If you see something more than once, check it more than once. The space below is for you to jot down notes about what you might have seen in the practice session.

Sitting and Movements

_____ 1. faces helpee squarely
_____ 2. looks at helpee
_____ 3. looks away from helpee
_____ 4. slouches or sits rigidly erect
_____ 5. sits in a relaxed manner
_____ 6. nods head
_____ 7. shows nervous mannerisms
_____ 8. shows distracting gestures
_____ 9. shows helpful gestures
_____ 10. touches the helpee
_____ 11. other_____

Responses

_____ 12. asks yes-no questions
_____ 13. asks more general questions
_____ 14. ask "why?" questions
_____ 15. asks a series of questions without pausing for an answer
_____ 16. asks probing questions (to get more information)
_____ 17. gives reassurance, encourages
_____ 18. expresses understanding
_____ 19. says "mm-hmm"
_____ 20. gives explanations

_____ 21. gives advice
_____ 22. gives moral judgments
_____ 23. responds to helpee feelings
_____ 24. responds to content statements
_____ 25. comments on helpee behavior
_____ 26. is silent
_____ 27. confronts
_____ 28. other_____

Voice

_____ 29. shaky and nervous voice
_____ 30. steady and reassuring voice
_____ 31. voice too loud
_____ 32. voice too soft
_____ 33. other_____

Helper Characteristics

_____ 34. patient
_____ 35. understanding
_____ 36. accepting
_____ 37. shows warmth and empathy
_____ 38. avoids discussing difficult issues
_____ 39. excessively curious
_____ 40. other_____

In general, the following are considered to be helpful and desirable responses: 1, 2, 5, 6, 9, 13, 16, 17, 18, 19, 23, 24, 25, 26, 30, 34, 35, 36, and 37.

Notes:

_____
Name of Observer-Evaluator

ROLE PLAY RATING SCALE

Date_____ Helper _____ Helpee _____

Watch the helper very carefully and check what you observe. If you see something more than once, check it more than once. The space below is for you to jot down notes about what you might have seen in the practice session.

Sitting and Movements

_____ 1. faces helpee squarely
_____ 2. looks at helpee
_____ 3. looks away from helpee

_____ 4. slouches or sits rigidly erect
_____ 5. sits in a relaxed manner
_____ 6. nods head
_____ 7. shows nervous mannerisms
_____ 8. shows distracting gestures
_____ 9. shows helpful gestures
_____ 10. touches the helpee
_____ 11. other_____

Responses

_____ 12. asks yes-no questions
_____ 13. asks more general questions
_____ 14. ask "why?" questions
_____ 15. asks a series of questions without pausing for an answer
_____ 16. asks probing questions (to get more information)
_____ 17. gives reassurance, encourages
_____ 18. expresses understanding
_____ 19. says "mm-hmm"
_____ 20. gives explanations

_____ 21. gives advice
_____ 22. gives moral judgments
_____ 23. responds to helpee feelings
_____ 24. responds to content statements
_____ 25. comments on helpee behavior
_____ 26. is silent
_____ 27. confronts
_____ 28. other_____

Voice

_____ 29. shaky and nervous voice
_____ 30. steady and reassuring voice
_____ 31. voice too loud
_____ 32. voice too soft
_____ 33. other_____

Helper Characteristics

_____ 34. patient
_____ 35. understanding
_____ 36. accepting
_____ 37. shows warmth and empathy
_____ 38. avoids discussing difficult issues
_____ 39. excessively curious
_____ 40. other_____

In general, the following are considered to be helpful and desirable responses: 1, 2, 5, 6, 9, 13, 16, 17, 18, 19, 23, 24, 25, 26, 30, 34, 35, 36, and 37.

Notes:

Name of Observer-Evaluator

RECOGNIZING CUES FOR AFFECTION OR HOSTILITY

1. A	11. H	21. A	31. H
2. A.	12. H	22. H	32. A
3. H	13. A	23. H	33. A
4. A	14. A	24. A	34. H
5. H	15. H	25. H	35. A
6. H	16. A	26. H	36. A
7. A	17. A	27. A	37. H
8. H	18. A	28. A	38. A
9. H	19. H	29. A	
10. A	20. H	30. A	

ROLE PLAY RATING SCALE

Date_____ Helper _____ Helpee _____

Watch the helper very carefully and check what you observe. If you see something more than once, check it more than once. The space below is for you to jot down notes about what you might have seen in the practice session.

Sitting and Movements

_____ 1.   faces helpee squarely
_____ 2.   looks at helpee
_____ 3.   looks away from helpee

_____ 4.   slouches or sits rigidly erect
_____ 5.   sits in a relaxed manner
_____ 6.   nods head
_____ 7.   shows nervous mannerisms
_____ 8.   shows distracting gestures
_____ 9.   shows helpful gestures
_____ 10. touches the helpee
_____ 11. other_____

Responses

_____ 12. asks yes-no questions
_____ 13. asks more general questions
_____ 14. ask "why?" questions
_____ 15. asks a series of questions without pausing for an answer
_____ 16. asks probing questions (to get more information)
_____ 17. gives reassurance, encourages
_____ 18. expresses understanding
_____ 19. says "mm-hmm"
_____ 20. gives explanations

_____ 21. gives advice
_____ 22. gives moral judgments
_____ 23. responds to helpee feelings
_____ 24. responds to content statements
_____ 25. comments on helpee behavior
_____ 26. is silent
_____ 27. confronts
_____ 28. other_____

Voice

_____ 29. shaky and nervous voice
_____ 30. steady and reassuring voice
_____ 31. voice too loud
_____ 32. voice too soft
_____ 33. other_____

Helper Characteristics

_____ 34. patient
_____ 35. understanding
_____ 36. accepting
_____ 37. shows warmth and empathy
_____ 38. avoids discussing difficult issues
_____ 39. excessively curious
_____ 40. other_____

In general, the following are considered to be helpful and desirable responses: 1, 2, 5, 6, 9, 13, 16, 17, 18, 19, 23, 24, 25, 26, 30, 34, 35, 36, and 37.

Notes:

Name of Observer-Evaluator

SUICIDE NOTES

In the space provided, indicate which of the notes you judge to be authentic.

	Your choice	*Correct Answer*	*Number Correct*
1	_____	_____	
2	_____	_____	
3	_____	_____	
4	_____	_____	
5	_____	_____	_____
6	_____	_____	
7	_____	_____	
8	_____	_____	
9	_____	_____	
10	_____	_____	_____

Total Correct _____

ROLE PLAY RATING SCALE

Date_____ Helper _____ Helpee _____

Watch the helper very carefully and check what you observe. If you see something more than once, check it more than once. The space below is for you to jot down notes about what you might have seen in the practice session.

Sitting and Movements

_____ 1. faces helpee squarely
_____ 2. looks at helpee
_____ 3. looks away from helpee
_____ 4. slouches or sits rigidly erect
_____ 5. sits in a relaxed manner
_____ 6. nods head
_____ 7. shows nervous mannerisms
_____ 8. shows distracting gestures
_____ 9. shows helpful gestures
_____ 10. touches the helpee
_____ 11. other_____

Responses

_____ 12. asks yes-no questions
_____ 13. asks more general questions
_____ 14. ask "why?" questions
_____ 15. asks a series of questions without pausing for an answer
_____ 16. asks probing questions (to get more information)
_____ 17. gives reassurance, encourages
_____ 18. expresses understanding
_____ 19. says "mm-hmm"
_____ 20. gives explanations

_____ 21. gives advice
_____ 22. gives moral judgments
_____ 23. responds to helpee feelings
_____ 24. responds to content statements
_____ 25. comments on helpee behavior
_____ 26. is silent
_____ 27. confronts
_____ 28. other_____

Voice

_____ 29. shaky and nervous voice
_____ 30. steady and reassuring voice
_____ 31. voice too loud
_____ 32. voice too soft
_____ 33. other_____

Helper Characteristics

_____ 34. patient
_____ 35. understanding
_____ 36. accepting
_____ 37. shows warmth and empathy
_____ 38. avoids discussing difficult issues
_____ 39. excessively curious
_____ 40. other_____

In general, the following are considered to be helpful and desirable responses: 1, 2, 5, 6, 9, 13, 16, 17, 18, 19, 23, 24, 25, 26, 30, 34, 35, 36, and 37.

_____

Notes:

_____
Name of Observer-Evaluator

ROLE PLAY RATING SCALE

Date_____ Helper _____ Helpee _____

Watch the helper very carefully and check what you observe. If you see something more than once, check it more than once. The space below is for you to jot down notes about what you might have seen in the practice session.

Sitting and Movements

_____ 1. faces helpee squarely
_____ 2. looks at helpee
_____ 3. looks away from helpee

_____ 4. slouches or sits rigidly erect
_____ 5. sits in a relaxed manner
_____ 6. nods head
_____ 7. shows nervous mannerisms
_____ 8. shows distracting gestures
_____ 9. shows helpful gestures
_____ 10. touches the helpee
_____ 11. other_____

Responses

_____ 12. asks yes-no questions
_____ 13. asks more general questions
_____ 14. ask "why?" questions
_____ 15. asks a series of questions without pausing for an answer
_____ 16. asks probing questions (to get more information)
_____ 17. gives reassurance, encourages
_____ 18. expresses understanding
_____ 19. says "mm-hmm"
_____ 20. gives explanations

_____ 21. gives advice
_____ 22. gives moral judgments
_____ 23. responds to helpee feelings
_____ 24. responds to content statements
_____ 25. comments on helpee behavior
_____ 26. is silent
_____ 27. confronts
_____ 28. other_____

Voice

_____ 29. shaky and nervous voice
_____ 30. steady and reassuring voice
_____ 31. voice too loud
_____ 32. voice too soft
_____ 33. other_____

Helper Characteristics

_____ 34. patient
_____ 35. understanding
_____ 36. accepting
_____ 37. shows warmth and empathy
_____ 38. avoids discussing difficult issues
_____ 39. excessively curious
_____ 40. other_____

In general, the following are considered to be helpful and desirable responses: 1, 2, 5, 6, 9, 13, 16, 17, 18, 19, 23, 24, 25, 26, 30, 34, 35, 36, and 37.

Notes:

_____
Name of Observer-Evaluator

BIBLE STUDY—SUGGESTED ANSWERS

In preparing this exercise, the author used the *New American Standard Bible*. All references are from the Book of Ephesians.

1. *Characteristics of People Helpers in the Body*
   (1:4) holiness, love
   (4:2) humility, gentleness, patience, forbearance
   (4:3) working to help people get along with each other
   (4:26) control of anger
   (4:32) kindness, tenderness, forgiving attitude

2. *Activities of People Helpers in the Body*
   (4:12) equipping the saints to serve and build up the body
   (4:15) speaking the truth in love, growing in maturity
   (4:22) casting off old habits
   (4:23) improving our minds (thoughts and attitudes)
   (4:24) becoming more God-like—righteous, holy, and truthful
   (4:25) eliminating untruths, speaking the truth
   (4:26) controlling anger
   (4:28) avoiding sin, working for others in need
   (4:29) controlling your tongue, speaking positive words
   (4:30) not grieving (bringing sorrow to) the Holy Spirit (by your style of life)
   (4:31) getting rid of bitterness, wrath, anger, clamor, slander
   (4:32) being kind, tender, forgiving

3. *Goals of People Helpers in the Body*
   (4:13) unity, knowledge, maturity in the body
   (4:14) stability
   (4:28) helping the needy

PERSONAL SURVEY

Good people helpers do not remain aloof and distant from others. Instead, they are compassionate, sensitive, and open with those in need. To help you examine your attitudes toward other people, please read the statements which appear below. Each is followed by a series of numbers. After reading each statement, *underline* the number which best identifies where you are on the scale. Then *draw a circle* around the number which best expresses where you would like to be.

A. In general, I am able to tell others that I really like and appreciate them.

Not at all able	1 2 3 4 5 6 7 8 9	Completely able

B. I am willing to discuss my feelings with others.

Not at all willing	1 2 3 4 5 6 7 8 9	Completely willing

C. I am able to tell a friend when I am angry about something he or she has done.

Not at all able	1 2 3 4 5 6 7 8 9	Completely able

D. I accept feedback about myself from others without responding in a defensive manner.

Completely able	1 2 3 4 5 6 7 8 9	Not at all able

E. I find it easy to relate to others.

Always find it easy	1 2 3 4 5 6 7 8 9	Never find it easy

F. I enjoy being with people.

Never enjoy it	1 2 3 4 5 6 7 8 9	Always enjoy it

G. I generally understand why I do what I do.

Never understand	1 2 3 4 5 6 7 8 9	Always understand

H. I am willing to give feedback to a friend when he or she is behaving in a way that bothers me.

Never
  willing   1 2 3 4 5 6 7 8 9   Always
                                                  willing

I. I am a person who trusts others.

Always
  trusts   1 2 3 4 5 6 7 8 9   Never
                                                  trusts

J. I feel free to discuss my problems and struggles with others.

Always feel
  free   1 2 3 4 5 6 7 8 9   Never feel
                                                  free

Your answers to these questions will be compared with others and discussed in the group meeting.

Group Member _____

empathy

warmth

genuineness

overall
helping   extremely   poor   fair   adequate   good   extremely
effectiveness   poor   good

Group Member _____

empathy

warmth

genuineness

overall
helping   extremely   poor   fair   adequate   good   extremely
effectiveness   poor   good

Group Member _____

empathy

warmth

genuineness

overall
helping   extremely   poor   fair   adequate   good   extremely
effectiveness   poor   good